IMAGES
of England

AROUND
CHARD, CREWKERNE
AND ILMINSTER

Crim | Chard

Wills's Lower

To Ilminster

To Avishays

To Crewkerne

from Honiton

Town Mill

Linney

from Harts Pit

To Burditch

To Axminster

To Forton

(1)
(2)
(3)
(4)
(5)
(6)
(7)
(8)
(9)
(10)
(11)
(12)

Foot Path

IMAGES
of England

AROUND
CHARD, CREWKERNE
AND ILMINSTER

Gerald Gosling
and Les Berry

TEMPUS

Chard once had two cinemas, the Regent in High Street, and the Cerdic in Fore Street, seen here. Both have long since closed.

Frontispiece: *Map of Chard, in around 1840, taken from the report of the proposed municipal boundary of the town.*

First published 2002

Tempus Publishing Limited
The Mill, Brimscombe Port,
Stroud, Gloucestershire, GL5 2QG

British Library Cataloguing in Publication Data.
A catalogue record for this book is available from the British Library.

ISBN 0 7524 2676 1

Typesetting and origination by Tempus Publishing Limited
Printed in Great Britain by Midway Colour Print, Wiltshire

Contents

A Rest Cure at CHARD.

STOLEN MOMENTS

Introduction

⟨⟩

On the other side of the coin, we once put a future
Chancellor of All England in the stocks.

Somerset is a county of many faces, and it rightly wears them all with an air of pride. Those faces range from the craggy, limestone stretches of the Mendip Hills and the world famous Cheddar Gorge; the wet and marshy flat lands of central Somerset and the equally flat coastal plain that looks out at Wales; the Quantock Hills, that run from the county town of Taunton towards that coast; the stunning Exmoor wastes that we have to share with Devon, and to our lovely south-west corner, where the flat lands that run to the north of the A303 change into the twisted countryside formed by a million years of the scouring of the upland plateau by a myriad of rivers and streamlets that hustle and bustle on their way to a wider life in the seas. It is not only Exmoor that we share with Devon. South-west Somerset and East Devon are so much alike that, if it was not for the sign that says 'Keep Devon Shipshape' just before the Fosse Way drops down Tytherleigh Hill, the first-time visitor would never know he had just crossed a county boundary.

South-west Somerset's largest town, and the nearest to Devon, is Chard, home to some 13,500 souls at the last count. There was a time when most of its inhabitants worked in one or another of the many mills and factories that were dotted around the town. So many, in fact, that it was claimed that more people per capita worked in factories in Chard than in any other town or city in the realm.

To the north of Chard is the lovely Minster town of Ilminster, to the east Crewkerne and the start of the Ham stone villages mostly, but not entirely so, built from the lovely, warm, brown stone dug since Roman times from the top of Ham Hill, a mini-range of hills rather than one hill, that looks out proudly over its large family. Around the three towns are some of the loveliest working villages in England.

They say that England's history is best sought in small places; after all, Sir Walter Raleigh – the country's greatest explorer-cum-sailor – was born in a tiny village as was Jack Churchill, later Duke of Marlborough, our greatest soldier.

In south-west Somerset you will find the inventor, if that is the right word, of powered flight; the man who discovered the source of the Nile; the hero of Cape St Vincent; the grave of the hero of Rorke's Drift; the first Englishman to set his eyes on Australia; the first women Cabinet Minister; a pioneer in artificial limbs and another in X-ray photography; a man who joined the Somerset Light Infantry as a private and, when he died (Field Marshals never retire), was a Field Marshal, and a world famous poet, born in America, but who so loved the land from which his forebears sprang that he became a Englishman and was buried in East Coker's St Michael's church where those forebears, as Kipling would have it 'are forty generations laid'. We also have the school where Sir Thomas Hardy, Nelson's captain, learnt the three Rs and, on the other side of the coin, we once put a future Chancellor of All England in the stocks. As if to compensate for that great man falling foul of Henry VIII, we have, in our midst, the most famous 'Henry' of the modern era.

But you will find more than that. You will find lovely villages lost down tiny, leafy lanes, thatch and stone, country pubs that still believe a ploughman ought to have a good lunch and not a minuscule crumb of cheese and one pickled onion half-hidden under a side salad, a lost canal and a lost railway line and, sadly, closed stations, timeless cricket grounds, contented cattle and contented people.

I was born at Chardstock in Devon, barely a couple of miles from Somerset, a village that owes it name to the fact that Chard's stock was once kept there. But I moved to Somerset (Tatworth) seven days later and, some sixty-eight years later, am still living in Chard.

I know the area like the back of my hand, but I am still more than grateful to Les Berry (a man of Chard I might add) and Gerald Gosling (who once worked there) for reminding me of so many of the evocative things of my life.

Frank Huddy, *Chard, 2002.*

ONE

Chard

'His family owes a life', snorted Judge Jeffries.

Man knew the Chard area long before the narrow confines of recorded time. He left his traces in the gravel beds of the nearby rivers, he left a Bronze Age awl and urn at South Chard and, most visible of all, he made his home on the hills that are dotted around south-west Somerset and east Devon, the area through which ran the boundary line behind which the Durotriges men glowered westward at their Dumnonii neighbours. To the south and south-east of Chard they lived on Hawkesdown Hill, Musbury Castle, Lamberts Castle, Pilsdon Pen and Lewesdon. To the west and north-west, they built their homes at Neroche, Membury Castle and Dumpton above Honiton. Even closer, an aerial survey has revealed a small settlement on Snowdon Hill. Man made his home on the top of the hills for safety's sake. Between them ran trackways, half man-made, half animal-made, some of which can still be traced today, including that which ran along Windwhistle towards Chard and onwards, keeping as much as possible to the hills, via Chardstock to Axminster.

The Romans came early to the West Country after their landing in Kent in AD 43. Around twelve years later they were at Exeter under Vespasian. If there is no evidence of Roman activity in Chard itself, the legions would have certainly known the area, the remains of one of their villas being discovered in a field at Higher Wadeford to the north of the town where the Somerset Archaeological Society unearthed parts of a mosaic pavement in 1886. It is now in Taunton Museum. Later, in the next field, a spear head and fibula were also found. Further evidence of Roman activity has been unearthed at Whitestaunton and South Chard,

Chard carnival, in around 1908, when the floats assembled in Victoria Avenue. Chard Town railway station can be seen in the background.

the latter as recently as 1967, when a considerable quantity of tiles and a thick wall and pavement were found.

And to the east and south of the town, the Fosse Way runs down from Windwhistle towards the valley of the Axe and the end of its long journey across England to reach the sea, probably at Seaton. The Fosse passes Chard at Perry Street, street being a corruption of *strata*, Latin for road. More evidence of Roman activity in the area is provided by the many coins found in several places in and around Chard, many of them by the eminent and worthy local Victorian historian Arthur Hull, and most of them in the region of Newhayes. Some think Chard's wide, arrow-straight main street might suggest Roman origins. It is, however, more likely to have been built that way after the disastrous fire of 1578 which means that apart from the church almost all of Chard dates from after that.

But Chard is essentially a Saxon settlement and claims are advanced that it takes its name from the West Saxon king, Cerdic, who landed in Britain in 495. Indeed, early references to the town include Cherde and Cerde (Domesday). Cerdic, a German according to William of Malmesbury, founded the royal house of Wessex and all future English monarchs apart from Harold II have his blood in their veins. Another school of thought has it that Chard is the site of the battle at Cerdicsford in 519 when Cerdic defeated the Romano-British. Others would have that the battle was fought at Charford near Salisbury. But not even George Pulman, who was never able to resist the chance to turn historical fact into a good yarn in his celebrated *Book of the Axe* (he has Cerdic landing at Charmouth in preference to Hampshire), goes as far as to agree with the suggestion that Chard takes its name from that far-off and misty Saxon warrior.

Be that as it may (or may not), Axminster is only five miles away and the Minster that gives that Devonshire town its name is reputed to have been founded as early as 786 by Cyneheard, king of Wessex from 756-7. Even earlier, in 614, the battle of Beandun, the Saxon victory that opened the way for their colonization of Devon, is said to have been fought at Bindon, high on the hills above the tiny village of Axmouth, another five miles on from Axminster. The facts point to Chard being settled well before the end of the seventh century.

Domesday says of Chard:

The same Bishop [Giso of Bath and Wells] holds Cerde. He also held it in the time of King Edward [the Confessor] and gelded for eight hides. The arable is twenty carucates [hides], and eleven servants, and twenty villiens, with fourteen ploughs, There is a mill yielding thirty pence, and twenty acres of meadow. Wood two miles long and four furlongs broad, and as much of pasture. On the same land a thane holds two hides, which cannot be separated from the church. The whole is worth sixteen pounds.

The Bishop of Bath and Wells would hold Chard until 1801, apart from a small break during the reign of Edward VI (1547-53) when it was 'given' to the king's uncle, the Duke of Somerset, for so-called services rendered in fighting against Scotland. In 1801 it was alienated to Lord Poulett for redemption of land tax. It was Bishop Jocelyn who was the father of the Borough of Chard when he granted the town a charter in 1235. Charles II's illegitimate son, the Duke of Monmouth, briefly raised the dust on Chard's streets after he landed at Lyme Regis and left there on 15 June, 1685, for Taunton and Sedgemoor. He arrived in Chard a day later after some half-hearted skirmishing at Axminster with the Devon Militia from the direction of Exeter, and the Somerset Militia, who soon ran away. The Duke's ragged army camped in a field on the outskirts of

Chard and it was probably then that the estimated 150 Chardians who fought for him joined the rebel army. But support from the gentry had been disappointing although one welcome arrival at Chard was John Speke, son of George Speke of Whitelackington, near Ilminster. Speke was promptly made a colonel, probably on the strength of the 'company of horse' that he brought with him. He escaped the retribution that followed by fleeing overseas; George, his father, and Lady Jennings, his sister who lived nearby at Burton Pynsent, got off with large fines. Not so lucky was his younger brother Charles who was hanged in Ilminster market place. His crime? He had been at his parents' home when George Speke welcomed the Duke and his followers at Whitelackington. 'His family owes a life,' snorted Judge Jeffries.

The rebel forces had another disappointment during their stay at Chard. A party that raided Forde Abbey in the hope of horses and arms, discovered that Edmund Prideaux, the owner, had left and all they found there were some coach horses. A rebel called Malachi Mallack is said to have drunk the Duke's health at Forde and later he gave false evidence against Edmund Prideaux who had been imprisoned in the Tower of London on a charge of high treason. Although there was no evidence against him he was disgracefully treated before being pardoned for a crime he did not commit. Mallack obtained a pardon for his perjured testimony against Prideaux and lived for many years after the event before dying at nearby Axminster in 1732.

Monmouth's proclamation as king was first mooted at Chard by Lord Grey but there was too much opposition and the idea was dropped for the time-being and rebels moved out to spend the next night at Ilminster, where they camped on the rich water meadows at Winterhay to the north of the town.

Monmouth was already being pursued. Lord John Churchill, with six troops of dragoons, had reached Chard via Bridport and Lyme Regis. He first attended the service on the Sabbath in St Mary's in Chard, and then went on to a brief skirmish when he caught up with some of Monmouth's men near Ashill. Churchill – later to become much more famous as the illustrious Duke of Marlborough – was on home ground when he marched through Axminster; he had been born at Ashe two miles away in 1750.

Chard featured prominently in the retribution that followed Monmouth's capture after the disastrous rout at Sedgemoor. When Judge

High Street, Chard, looking down towards Fore Street and the Corn Exchange in the background.

Jeffreys arrived in the town, according to tradition at least, he hanged twelve rebels on a tree outside the grammar school, which must have been a welcome distraction from Latin. Another school of thought claims that the executions took place where the Tesco store now stands. Local tradition also has it that the judge stayed at the Choughs in High Street, a handsome building of squared flint stones from the nearby Snowdon Hill quarries with Ham stone dressing and attractive mullioned windows. Now a public house, it dates from around 1600 and has some unusual plaster work in one of the upper rooms, the pattern including dragons, roses and fleur-de-lis.

Jeffreys is said to have delivered what passed for justice in the Manor Court House, an Elizabethan building behind Waterloo House almost opposite the Guildhall, but there has to be some doubt here. The Court House is reached by a passageway from the main street. Waterloo House is actually a group of buildings dating from around the same time as the Manor Court House, its lower fronts having long since been taken over as shops, including Norrington's, a well-known Chard ironmonger's business who once delivered paraffin and other oils around the surrounding districts.

Chard in 1850, according to George Pulman, consisted of four main streets meeting at right angles, with the continuation of High Street and Fore Street praised as 'very good for a country town being wide, straight and nearly a mile long.' High Street had been much improved in 1831 by

13

the removal of the shambles in front of the Poulett Arms, a now closed inn where a medical centre stands today. The old market house, which stood in front of the George Hotel, followed three years later and in June of the same year the old Guildhall was also demolished. Usually referred to as the New Work by local residents of the time, the Guildhall was of uncertain age, the earliest reference to it being in a deed of 1570 when it was said to have been used for municipal purposes, but its windows indicate that it had been originally built for a religious purpose. George Pulman suggests it may have been a chapel of ease but its close proximity to St Mary's would probably rule out this theory.

Both the Guildhall and the market house was replaced in 1835 when the Corn Exchange was built in Fore Street, almost opposite the site of the latter. The new building contained the town hall and council chambers in the upper part with meat and other stalls below. The meat stalls were certainly still in use as such as late as the years immediately prior to the Second World War. In 1966, after renovations which saw the move of the old air-raid siren to the fire station, the Corn Exchange officially became the Guildhall again on Thursday 10 March. Almost all of the building, except the offices facing the road, was demolished in 2002 and rebuilt.

Around 1840 an Act of Parliament to increase the municipal boundary of Chard said that at the last census (1831) there were 489 families in the town and a total population of 2,511 living in 450 houses. The grip that

The George Hotel, Chard, c. 1900.

Fore Street, Chard, c. 1900. The offices of Mitchell, Toms & Company, Chard's brewers, are on the right. They moved there from a building just out of view on the right, which was taken into the post office in 1902.

the manufacturing trade had taken on the town at the time was reflected by the fact that out of the 489 houses, the families of as many as 374 of them were chiefly employed in trade, manufacture or handicraft, and only nineteen of them by families working in the farming community.

The arrival of the Chard Canal should have been a godsend to the mills and factories and a shot in the arm to the town's business community. But procrastination, and opposition from local landowners, meant that Chard's canal was built far too late. It lasted just twenty-six years, its closure in 1868 coming hard on the heels of the arrival of the railway that had reached Chard a few years earlier. Originally the plan had been one of many suggested to build a canal linking the Bristol and English Channels, usually from around the mouth of the River Parret and the Axe at Seaton. Other suggestions included a link with the Tiverton Canal and the River Exe.

The first real moves began in 1769 when Robert Whitworth, an engineer of repute, was engaged to explore the area looking for a possible route between Langport and the mouth of the Devonshire Axe. Nothing was done but he came back for a second look twenty years on. Later the great Thomas Telford was brought in to survey a possible line that ended at Beer, near Seaton. The last section of this would have used tub boats.

In the end a canal was built linking Chard with the Bridgwater and Taunton Canal at Creech St Michael. Work started in 1835 at Wrantage and, by May 1841, the canal had reached Ilminster amidst scenes of

15

The Corn Exchange (Guildhall) which, when it was built in 1835, replaced an older building containing the town hall and council chambers above the meat and other stalls below. Sometimes known as the Guildhall, after a building that stood at the junction of Fore Street and High Street, it officially became the Guildhall in 1966 after renovations, although older generations of Chardians still refer to it as the Corn Exchange.

much jollification. Soon after, it arrived at Chard, where the still existing reservoir was built specifically to provide water for the project, although Lord Poulett, the lord of the manor, secured the rights to fish there and sail boats on it.

From the high land to the west of the town, two small springs send their waters down to run together on either side of the main street. There are schools of thought, including many Somerset county guide books, that claim that the left-hand stream, via Chard Reservoir and the River Isle, finally reaches the Bristol Channel. The right-hand stream turns south to meet the Axe and then the English Channel. The latter stream undoubtedly does reach the English Channel, joining an anonymous brook that reaches the Axe below Chilson Common. Whether the other stream reaches River Isle is another matter. Another claim made on Chard's behalf is that it is the highest town in Somerset: the western edges of the town do just touch the 160-metre contour and a good part of it is above the 130 metres line, which means a large part of Chard stands on land above 400 feet.

The Chard Railway opened in 1863 almost instantly killing off much of the canal's trade, an Act of Parliament finally closing the canal around February 1868. The line of the canal can still be seen, although, near Ilton, the RAF Merrifield airfield was built on top of it. The reservoir still exists as a nature reserve. Another 'left-over' from the canal's early days is the Furnham Hotel, the only successful one of several applicants for spirit licenses among the many who hoped to make a killing from the bargees and the other trade the canal was expected to bring. Bargees no longer call, but the Furnham Hotel continues to be one of Chard's favourite watering places. In time the canal basin was filled in and the site used for industrial purposes and it was there in 1946 that B.G. Wyatt Ltd moved from Ilminster where it had started business in 1923. Their mill was one of the first things to catch the eye as you approached Chard from the north and 'Try It From Wyatt' became quite a popular catch-phrase at the time. To help house employees, Mr Wyatt had the first two houses built in the town after the Second World War in Furnham Crescent by local builder Charlie Turner. The first man to move in was Jack Helliar who ended his forty-eight years with the company as office manager. By that time Crosfields had taken over the business, and it was taken over again by Spillers Ltd and the business ended its Chard life as Dalgety Agriculture. Closed around 1996, a DIY store has since been built on the site.

Dalgety's animal feeding stuff mills in Furnham Road shortly before closure around 1996. The buildings were demolished and a DIY store now occupies the site.

One of the first motor cars seen in Chard belonged to Mr H.S. Boden, the owner of Boden's Mill, who drove it to watch the play-off for the Perry Street and District Football League championship in 1908 between his mill's team and Combe Wanderers on the Holyrood Mills ground. *The Chard & Ilminster News* said that, 'Among the thousand people at the play-off on the Holyrood Mills ground was Mr H.S. Boden and his three sons who caused a ripple of excitement when they arrived in his car.'

But almost certainly the oldest sporting organization in Chard is the cricket club which, according to Chard Union Gazette, was formed in May 1841 for 'the practice of that truly English game – Cricket'. At the time, cricket was the preserve of the better classes, and would remain so until well after the First World War. Football, born in the public schools and the officers mess however, was hijacked by the workers soon after the FA Cup was started in 1872.

Cricket's early home in the town was at Lordsleaze where the pitch was obviously not up to today's standards. This led to a search for another ground and in 1883 the club merged with the Standard Cricket Club who played at Crimchard, and a move was made to the club's present home at George Field.

Holyrood Mills Football Club 1910/11, the season they finished third in the Perry Street & District League. One of the original member clubs of that league, and champions in 1904/05 and 1906/07, they disbanded after the 1920/21 season when the new Chard Town team began to take the best players from the mill sides.

Boden & Company football club. The date on the ball looks like 1907 but this is unlikely to be correct. The Perry Street League's original championship trophy was a cup, but Bodens had not won any trophies at that time. However, from the following season they finished first three years in a row and also became the first side from south-west Somerset to win the Somerset Junior Cup.

Chard Cricket Club really took off when the Dening brothers arrived on the scene. William, Herbert and Ernest Dening, the sons of Mr S.H. Dening, the owner of the Crimchard Engineering Works dominated the club from the 1890s down to the years immediately before the Second World War. It may have been an autocratic domination, but it was also a benevolent one, the family helping considerably in keeping the accounts in the black. Another generous patron of the club was Charles Small, the owner of the lace factory at Perry Street who also acted as scorer. He married Elsie Mary Dening and he used his connections with the lace trade in Nottingham to bring teams to Chard who, although thinly disguised as Mr C.E. Small's XI, were in fact almost all professionals with the Nottinghamshire county side. This led to such well-known cricketers as J. Ironmonger, E. Alletson, Jack Gunn, W.T. Taylor, T. Forrester. A.T.C. Worsely and A.W. Carr, who one day captained England against Australia, playing at the George Field.

Out of all the businesses associated with Chard the name of Dening is the best known, the former farm machinery engineers selling products all over the world. In the early years it was Wightman & Denning, John Wightman, a local farmer having bought a smithy in Old Town in 1828 where he made farm machinery and ploughs. By 1842 he was in partnership with Charles Dening, an ironmonger in the town. Wightman

Part of the workforce at Phoenix Engineering Company in Combe Street, Chard. The business began as the Phoenix Iron Works in 1839 and was bought by Thomas John Jennings in 1891. Still here today, Phoenix exports its goods to over 150 countries.

retired in 1867 and the firm became known as Dening & Co., moving in 1881 into premises in Crimchard that had been occupied by James Budgett's rope and twine works. By then Charles Dening had been dead for a year and his son Samuel was running the business. He added such lines as kitchen ranges, iron garden seats, water troughs and, for a spell, cast iron grave markers and crosses up to 8ft high. Some of the latter can still be seen in graveyards throughout the West Country and further afield. Another important line in Victorian times was a night soil box.

The family were not just the major employers in the town. As was so often the case with industrialists in most towns of any size, they played a big part in the civic life of Chard. Charles Dening was on the Borough Council for forty-seven years and was an alderman and also served as mayor. His son Samuel was mayor no less than eleven times and died in office, and his son, Herbert (Bert), was mayor for six successive years. Bert, and his two brothers, William and Ernest, were associated with Chard cricket club from 1886, when William became secretary, until 1962, when Herbert stood down as President. All three played the game and played it well and all three remained as bachelors.

Bert became managing director on the death of his father in 1919, the three brothers remaining in charge until 1937 when, ninety-five years later, three generations of the family had successfully steered the business. All three retired, although Bert continued on the Board of the new business which traded under the name of Dening & Co. (1937) Ltd.

During the Second World War aircraft parts were made for the London firm of F.J. Edwards as well as the farming machine lines which were also vital to the war effort. After the war the firm ran into financial difficulties when a £1 million pound order from Argentina was cancelled because of the 'corned-beef war' between that country and Great Britain. At the time much of the order had been completed and the firm went into voluntary liquidation in 1950 and the company was wound up the following year. Bayer-Peacock of Manchester acquired the premises, trading there as Dening of Chard Ltd. They sold off the Crichard works which eventually fell foul of the developers' maw. The 'bottom' factory, the Somerset Works, which had originally been built during the war as assembly works for farming machinery made in Australia, carried on making farm machinery until 1965 and spare parts until 1974. By 1966, however, the firm had become Space Decks Ltd and the name of Dening vanished from Chard's industrial story after 124 years.

The lace trade played a prominent part in Chard's industrial story, arriving there around 1819 after Luddites had driven Messrs Heathcote & Boden and other firms out of Loughborough to Tiverton. By the 1830s the firm of William Oram & Co. had started making lace in Mill Lane on a site later occupied by Wheatley and Riste which, in turn, was purchased by Bodens & Co. around 1875. Bodens stayed there until 1938 when it was closed and the premises obtained by Dualloys, manufacturers of aircraft parts during the Second World War. Later they turned to manufacturing plain bearings. Later still, Dualloys changed their name to Glacier Metal Company Ltd and moved to Winterhaye in Ilminster. The mill's strikingly tall chimney was taken down on safety grounds in the 1980s and the whole building converted into small industrial units.

The lace making firm of Gifford, Fox & Co. Ltd was started in Holyrood Mills in 1850 by Mr J.B. Gifford, who was followed by his son, Col. J.W. Gifford, a friend of Scott of the Antarctic, and, in turn, by his grandson, Col. R.E. Gifford. In 1956 the business was acquired by Black Bros & Boden Ltd based in Nottingham and the circle was completed. The name of Boden that had vanished from Chard in 1938, came back once more into the town's industrial picture.

Much shorter lived, and now only remembered by an ever-decreasing number of Chardians, was Ensor & Southcombe's glove factory, which was opened in the early 1930s in Victoria Avenue at premises now occupied by a fish and chip shop. The owners also had glove factories and

Some of the staff at Ensor & Southcombe's glove factory in Victoria Avenue, Chard, around 1938. From left to right, back row: Doug Broom, Ivor Cooksleigh, Jack Richards, Harry Sibley, Doug Hounsell. Front row: Ken Stoodley, Dick Potter, Cyril Stoodley, Doug Tucker, Noel Page.

tanneries at Tintinhull and Milborne Port, from where the gloves were cut and taken to Chard for stitching. At first only women were employed at Chard but later a mostly masculine cutting staff was added. There were also considerable numbers of 'out workers'.

During the Second World War the factory made drivers' and dispatch riders' gauntlet gloves for the military and also some ski gloves. After the war the factory returned full-time to making mostly men's leather dress gloves which were supplied to superior stores and the retail trade and, at one stage, over 100 people were employed in the factory or on 'out work'. Later the changes in fashion – when many men stopped wearing gloves and those that did turned to cheap imports – the death knell of much of the glove industry that had been centred in the Yeovil area for many years was sounded. Ensor & Southcombe's Chard factory's work force was reduced to two cutters and later, when Mr Taunton the manager took over the factory, there was only one part-time cutter left. Later still the business moved to the old High Street School and was closed around the end of the 1960s.

One of Chard's more successful self-made sons, although he was actually born at Tatworth in 1916, was Jack Baulch, a larger-than-life entrepreneur who started his working life as a learner-boy at the Central Motor Works in East Street at the age of fourteen. Before the Second World War he bought the Turnpike Garage on the A30 beyond Snowdon Hill where he started a motor coach business known as Chard & District Motor Services. From there he ran bus services from Chard to such small hamlets as Wambrook, Whitestaunton, Chaffcombe and Cudworth where there were very few travel facilities. He also 'delivered' some of the workforce for Chard's factories and ran tours to many of the West Country's seaside attractions such as Bude, Seaton, Weston-super-Mare and Weymouth.

The business was sold and became Wessex Motors, Jack changing direction and going into the haulage business. He started the Chard Transport Company with two lorries and within five years was running fourteen lorries out of a depot in East Street. He was a keen sportsman, especially where football was concerned, and his thirty-year association with Chard Town AFC saw him serve as both chairman and President before becoming a life member. He served as chairman to the Perry Street and District Football League from 1967-71 and became a director of Yeovil Town and also acted as a scout for Bristol City.

But Chard's most famous son was either John Stringfellow, the inventor of powered flight, or James Gillingham, a pioneer of artificial limbs. Incidentally, Stringfellow manufactured leg calipers for Gillingham. There might be room for argument there, but there can be none over the question of the town's most famous daughter, Miss Margaret Bonfield.

Miss Bonfield was born in the town and went on to become an MP and the first woman to serve in the Cabinet. In 1918 Constance Markievicz became the first woman to be elected to the British Parliament. She had been sentenced to death for her part in the Dublin Easter Rising of 1916, a sentence later commuted to life imprisonment, and she was later released under an amnesty after running her campaign from inside Holloway prison. Like the first woman to

Margaret Bonfield, the first woman to serve in the Cabinet, doing so in 1930 as Minister of Labour in Ramsay McDonald's minority administration.

actually take her seat in the House, Nancy Astor, who became MP for Plymouth in 1919 when her husband succeeded his father in the House of Lords, Markievicz was not interested in women's rights. Nor was Margaret Bonfield who, after two other women entered Parliament after by-elections in 1921 and 1923, was one of the five women elected at the 1923 general election. In her case it was at the third attempt at Northampton (she later sat for Wallsend). She was more interested in workers' right than those of the 'gentle sex' (her maiden speech was on unemployment). She came from a solid Labour background, her father being a lace-maker in Chard and she started her own working life as a shop assistant. Attracted early into the Trade Union Movement, Margaret Bonfield joined the Shop Assistants' Union and rose through its ranks to become its general secretary. At the time of her election to Parliament she was the chairman of the TUC's General Council. Similar promotion was to follow in Parliament where almost immediately she was appointed as Under-Secretary of State at the Ministry of Labour in Ramsay McDonald's first (1924) administration. She reached cabinet status six years later when she was appointed to the post of Minister of Labour in Ramsay McDonald's 1929 minority administration. She was blamed for the lack of unemployment relief, really due to a lack of money, and attacked by both sides of the House. The Left claimed that she was not doing enough, the Right thought she was doing too much. She lost office when McDonald formed a National Government in 1931. Miss Bonfield wanted nothing to do with him or it and, after, losing her seat in 1931, she resumed her work in the Trade Union movement. Her brother was active on Chard Town Council as late as the immediate post-war years.

Strictly speaking, John Stringfellow was not a son of Chard, being born at Attercliffe, Sheffield in 1799. He was apprenticed to a bobbin-net lace manufacturer in Nottingham in 1815 arriving at Chard in 1819 when he was sent there to install machines in Mill Lane, presumably for Bodens. He was to play an important part in the life of the town which he served for fourteen years as a Liberal councillor and he was also a church warden and a burgess. During that time he was the man behind the introduction of gas street lighting in Chard. He obtained three houses in a terrace at the top of High Street where a plaque giving brief details of the man can be seen today on the wall facing the road. He built a workshop there and went into business as an engineer and, including aeronautics among his many interests, he gained the sobriquet of 'The Flying Man'.

Prospect House, Combe Street, Chard, around 1912, at the time the home of James Gillingham (1839-1924) a native of the town who learnt his trade under his mother at the Golden Boot shoe shop in High Street. He was a pioneer in artificial limbs.

Much of the research into flight was done with William Henson, a friend who had many irons in the engineering fire, including a breech-loading cannon and an ice machine. The association of both men with Chard was remembered in the naming of a Henson Park and a Stringfellow Crescent in the post-war council estate of Old Town. Henson later went to America and died there in 1888. Henson's reputation, definitely, and Stringfellow's possibly, is better known in the United States than in his own country. Indeed the first question many American soldiers asked when they arrived in Chard during the Second World War was, 'Where is Stringfellow's grave?'. They would be taken to the cemetery in Combe Street and shown the grave with its model of the 'first plane' on the iron railings that surround it.

Stringfellow still hankered over powered flight and in 1848, after many setbacks including a failed attempt at a 'first flight' on Bewley Down to the south-west of Chard, he finally etched his name for all time in the history of flight when 'he flew his machine some fifteen yards inside a large and empty room in Holyrood Lace Mills.' Later, in London, in a large marquee and before a distinguished audience of 'scientific gentlemen' a flight of forty yards was achieved. And all this fifty years before the Wright brothers finally achieved manned flight at Kittyhawk, North Carolina, in 1903.

Stringfellow's House, High Street, Chard, which John Stringfellow (1799-1883) built, complete with a factory at the rear, soon after his arrival in the town in 1820.

There is much to admire among the handsome buildings that line Chard's main thoroughfare, none more so than the grammar school towards the foot of Fore Street. It was built in 1583 as a private residence for William Symes of Painsford just after the great fire of 1578. A grammar school under twelve trustees and with accommodation for the master was founded there in 1671 and among its pupils was Thomas Wakely, the medical and social reformer and founder and editor of *The Lancet,* who was born just over the Somerset-Devon border at Membury in 1795. Inside there is a lot of good plaster, but some damage was done by a fire in 1727. There was a disastrous fire at the school just after the Second World War when a 1932 extension to the building was gutted, the fire believed to have been started in the prefects' study. Immediately above the study was a dormitory with thirty boys sleeping there, twenty of them were led out of the building by Mr Cadman, a teacher, but the other ten had to be lowered to safety by fire-escape slings. Sadly, all the school trophies and many historic pictures were lost. The town rallied around the school, there being many offers of temporary accommodation from householders, and breakfast that morning was served to the pupils and staff on time – in the canteen at Messrs Brecknell Willis & Company's factory. Probably even more enjoyable was the lunch that day which was brought from White's fish

Chard grammar school, roughly 1901. The buildings, rear centre, form an imposing background to what appears to be a Chard carvival procession making its way from Victoria Avenue via East Street into Fore Street. In the distance can be seen the bell turret of Furnham church.

and chip shop in Boden Street where the White family would look after the town's needs in that direction for well over half a century.

During the Second World War, the American servicemen, stationed mainly in Furnham Road, soon discovered the delights of a 'skate and two.' So much so that, when Mr White told them that he could not serve them one day because of a shortage of potatoes, they brought some sacks of their own for him and he never went short of spuds again. Fifty years later one of the soldiers came back to Chard and one of his first ports of call was White's chippy.

After the pupils had tucked in to their fish and chips they slept that night in the Drill Hall using beds and blankets which were supplied by the borough council. Over £800 worth of text books had been lost, but members of the staff journeyed to London and Oxford for replacements.

Outside the school, a particularly handsome gas light standard, one of the town's best-known landmarks, vanished in the interests of road safety. Back in 1903 a trough had been placed beside it to mark the death of William Hussey, who drowned while trying to save his friend Ernest Jones, who was in difficulties in Chard Reservoir. Unlike the gas standard, the trough was saved and removed to the Millfield Industrial estate.

Next above the school, Monmouth House was built as a private residence but used in later years (certainly post Second World War) as the headmaster's home. Next door again, Essex House has many murals inside, one of them said to have been painted by French prisoners during the Napoleonic Wars. Both buildings have iron railings which, along with those around St Mary's church, escaped the attentions of wartime salvage drives.

In the middle of Fore Street – almost opposite the Guildhall, and what is now Lloyds Bank – the Chard Arms Hotel was built in 1849 when it was said to be 'an establishment complete with every convenience for the accommodation of the commercial traveler and families visiting the Western Counties.' In later years Chard's popular local paper, *The Chard & Ilminster News*, was housed in offices just inside the archway which led to the hotel's stables.

After William Forster MP, a Bridport man, masterminded Gladstone's Education Act of 1870, a new school was built at Ivy Green on the edge of the town on the Axminster road in 1874 with room for 400 pupils – 114 boys, 114 girls and 172 infants. The new school had been designed by John Wightman, a partner of the Chard firm of Wightman & Dening, and built at a cost of £930 by James Hawker, a local builder. Much of the stone came from the Chard Quarry which closed soon afterwards. This school closed before the Second World War, but it was remembered some years later by Mr R.W. Quick who started teaching there as

Chard Southend (Ivygreen) Girls' Council School, group 1, around 1900.

monitor teacher at the age of thirteen when he was paid three shillings (15p) a week and taught a class of twenty-five. In all his teaching career lasted forty-seven years before he retired in 1948 as headmaster of Bishop Hull's Council School.

When he started teaching at the school in 1901 all the classes were seated in one long room, at long desks with no backs. The two lowest classes did all their work on slates which, he told *Pulman's Weekly News* on the occasion of his retirement, 'were cleaned in different ways – hygienic or otherwise.' At the time the emphasis was on the 3Rs, but there were other lessons including history, geography and object lessons. But there was no physical training or organized games. The children left school at the age of thirteen, or earlier if they could pass a Labour Examination, some working at the Chard lace factory as 'half-timers' having been allowed to leave and go to work at the age of eleven.

When the school closed, its pupils were transferred to Holyrood school in Duck Lane, where the infants and the senior pupils were taught, which meant that pupils started at Duck Lane, moved to the junior school in High Street, and then went back to Duck Lane to finish their education. Holyrood school still takes the infants, but the High Street school was demolished to make way for Hellier Road, the new link road that takes traffic away from Combe Street. The pupils moved to the new school at Zembard Lane.

Returning to the Ivy Green school – usually called the Southend school – soldiers, British and later American, were stationed there during the Second World War. Then the pencil manufacturing firm of L. & C. Hardtmuth (Great Britain) Ltd, who had been making pencils in Austria for 200 years, moved into the premises as well as others in Combe Street in 1946. The pencil produced at Chard was called the Koh-i-Nor after the world famous diamond, the advertising line being that their pencil was the 'jewel of pencils'. Pencils are no longer made in Chard, the Ivy Green school having been converted for accommodation purposes into eight flats known as South End Mews

Before Dr Beeching wielded his infamous axe, Chard had two railway stations barely half a mile apart. Chard Town, the first to be built, was served by the three-mile branch line from Chard Road (Chard Junction from 1872) on the old London and South-West Railway's Waterloo-Exeter line. That station was built in 1860, and Chard Town itself was opened on 8 May 1863 when the whole town was *en-fête* with all the shops closing, the church bells being rung and anyone of importance wining and dining in a marquee near the station. The men who had actually done the work, seventy-five navvies, sat down to a hot meal at the Red Lion which stood in East Street at the time.

A ticket from Chard Town to the junction cost four pence, and it was possible to buy a first class return ticket from Chard to Waterloo for just over fifteen shillings.

Chard Joint station, which was later renamed Chard Central, actually stood beside the old canal basin and was opened in September 1866, and it connected the town with the GWR main line at Taunton. There were intermediate stations – or halts – at Donyatt, Ilminster, Ilton, Hatch Beauchamp and Thornfalcon. Unlike the LSWR between Chard Town and its junction, the Chard Joint branch was broad gauge until July 1891 when it was the last of the GWR's lines to be converted to standard gauge. Only then were trains able to run the whole line between Taunton and Chard Road.

The first stage in the ultimate closure of the lines arrived in 1962 when passenger services between Chard and Taunton were closed, although goods services continued for another two years. In April 1966, 103 years after its opening, the Chard Junction branch also closed, although the mainline station remained open until 7 March 1967 to cater for the nearby milk factory's trade.

Nothing remains of the Chard Town station, the site now being occupied by Tesco but the Chard Central station buildings still remain. Apart from them the only real reminder of Chard's age of steam is the Chard Road Hotel which was opened to cater for the railway trade at Chard Junction. It stands on the other side of the road where it stared straight down the branch line towards Chard. Its position put it in jeopardy in 1939 when an engine with two coaches failed to stop and smashed through the buffers and fence, crossed the road, and ended up in the hotel's forecourt. Later (1961), during shunting at Chard Central station, some loose trucks escaped and ran the three-mile length of the branch line before breaking through a pair of buffers and the station fence, snapping off an electricity pole and crossing the main road. There they smashed through a gate before coming to rest on the forecourt of the hotel. Happily there were no casualties but a bus shuttle service was operated between the junction and Chard. In addition many people in the area had their electricity supply cut off for some time. The licensee,

Mr Harold Fowler and his wife, were out shopping at the time but their eleven-year-old daughter Hilary was playing in the garden but was well away from danger. The hotel survived the railway closures but, perhaps sadly, has changed its name to the Three Counties Hotel, no doubt a reference to the fact that Somerset, Devon and Dorset all meet a mile or so to the south.

Although for many years Chard's mail was brought to the town by rail, it had originally arrived on horseback from Salisbury. Known as a post boy even if he was over sixty, a man left Salisbury daily to service the towns along the A30, including Crewkerne and Chard, as far as Exeter. Later, in the wake of the road improvements brought about by the Turnpike Trusts, Chard (and Crewkerne) were served by a mail coach. Previously, mail-coach traffic to the West Country had looped south of Somerset because of the hilly nature of the A30 west of Salisbury and gone on to Exeter via Blandford Forum, Dorchester, Bridport and Axminster.

In 1831 the post office was in Market Place but, by 1842, it was in Holyrood Street, and later it moved to a prominent position on the southern side of the Fore Street-Holyrood Street junction. It was there, in 1908, that Chard was joined to the national telephone service. In the mid-1960s the post office moved down towards the bottom of Fore Street on part of the site of the old cattle market. Recently it crossed the road and moved further back up Fore Street.

At first, letters for the villages around Chard went mostly by foot post, outgoing mail from those villages being handed in at a receiving house. Since the eighteenth century there had been a charge of one penny to cover the cost of the journey to the post office and the letter was usually, but not always, hand-stamped to show that the penny had been paid. Not unnaturally the system was called the Chard Penny Post. It was not unique to Chard; almost every small town that had a post office served its smaller neighbours and, thus, there was a Bridport Penny Post, a Bridlington Penny Post and so on.

Mail either reached or left Chard by four different types of posts: London letters, country letters, cross-post letters and bye-letters. The first group is self explanatory, being letters that went direct to or from the capital. Country letters passed through London on their way to their final destination, say Chard to Canterbury. As the name suggests, a cross-post was one that went 'across country' and did not touch London on its way from one provincial town to another; Dorchester-Bristol, Exeter-Cardiff and many others. Bye-letters travelled along the main coach runs without getting as far as London, from Chard, say, to Salisbury or Andover.

Once the letter arrived at Chard from the receiving houses, the cost of conveying it to its final destination was calculated by the number of miles it had to travel. Before the introduction of the Universal Penny Post and the postage stamp the charges were considerable although the rate tended to be lowered for longer distances. Thus, although a letter from Chard to Yeovil cost about five pence, one to London cost only ten pence.

Thanks in no small way to Christmas cards, the image in most people's minds when they think of the coaching era is that of the romantic mail coach speeding its way though the snow-covered country with horns blaring ahead to warn the gate keeper to open his toll gates and help the King's mail on its unhindered way. But they were only a small part of England's coaching story. Before the advent of the railway system, that part of the nation's commerce which was not carried on the canals nor by the main coaching system travelled by the back roads and the carriers. These carriers and their horse-drawn carts were the life blood of rural England's commerce. They plodded out of towns such as Chard until after the First World War when motorized transport finally killed them off. The countryside was crisscrossed by carrying routes that had evolved over the years. Most towns were connected with their immediate neighbours and enjoyed being on one or more long-distance routes. There were as many as ten coaches a day passing through Chard in 1842. The Devonport mail left daily from the George at half-past twelve on its way to London and, on Wednesdays, Fridays and Sundays another coach belonging to Russell & Co. left from Mrs Cross's in Market Place. Russell's also ran a coach from Market Place to Exeter on Tuesdays, Fridays and Sundays and there were other carriers plying regularly between Chard and Axminster, Lyme Regis, Bristol and Bath, Taunton, Barnstaple and Plymouth. Most carriers took passengers as well. Regular changes of horses were made at coaching inns and, with an average speed of three or four miles-per-hour, it was often a long and tiring journey in all kinds of weather.

The tonnage of goods arriving in Chard must have been considerable. Around the middle of the nineteenth century there were as many as eighteen boot and shoe makers listed in the town and, and although leather would have been cured locally, much of it would have needed to be transported. There were also six blacksmiths, three book shops, all

Messrs Brown & Cuff were saddlers and harness makers in Fore Street, Chard, and were still in existence as Cuff's immediately before the Second World War.

supplying stationery and acting as printers, two tinsmiths, four butchers, six carpenters, two china and glass dealers, three chemists, three clothiers, eight fire insurers who would not have needed the carriers, nor would the three hairdressers very often, eight grocers, who would, two watch and clock repairers and two wheelwrights. Add to that the bakers, millers, and at least one confectioner, coach builder, rubber manufacturer, pawnbroker, brick maker (in Furnham), rope maker, sail manufacturer, tallow chandler, lace machinery manufacturer, basket maker, wool dyer, millwright, an engineer in the High Street by the name of John Stringfellow, and as many as fifteen beer retailers, and you have a thriving and virtually self sufficient little town.

With fifteen beer retailers, Chard's 2,100-odd inhabitants (140 for each of the fifteen) were hardly likely to go for long without a drink. There were also two wine and spirit dealers and at least eighteen public houses, White's Directory of 1842 listing the Bell, Choughs, Crown, Dolphin, Furnham Hotel, the King's Arms and King's Head on opposite corners in Old Town, the London Inn, New Inn, Poulett's Arms, Red Lion, Rising Sun (at Chardleigh Green), Ship, White Hart and the White Horse. There have been many casualties including the Victoria Hotel (as recent as 2002), the Masons Arms, and the delightfully named Live And Let Live Inn that once thrived in Old Town.

TWO

Chard's Villages

It took 40,000 gallons of cream, which took 600,000 gallons
of milk from 200,000 cows, to produce 100 tons of butter.

Pulman's Weekly News

Heading south from Chard towards Devonshire, Tatworth lies mostly off the main road and is a place where the unsuspecting visitor could easily get lost in a maze of back streets and lanes. It is closely connected with South Chard and Perry Street, once separate parishes but now all lumped together, along with Chard Junction, to form the combined parish of Tatworth. Its church is dedicated to St John the Evangelist, a recent structure, having been built as a mission chapel in 1851 and becoming the parish church fourteen years later. Outside, one of the village's more prominent features was the fir tree that was planted in 1887 to mark Queen Victoria's Golden Jubilee. It became the village's unofficial meeting place, especially for courting couples, but road improvements finally led to its removal in 1969 when not even a petition to HM Government could stop the axe falling. It was first lopped, then felled, before almost the entire village who jeered the workers throughout.

One old Tatworth custom that has not been felled is the annual candle auction for Stowell Mead, a watercress meadow in the village which is auctioned in the Poppe Inn, the successful bid being the last one made before an inch of tallow candle burns out.

The ground for the church and the stone for its construction, was a gift of the lord of the manor, Earl Poulett. The organ, which arrived in 1860, was a gift of John Payne, the owner of the lace mill at Perry Street at the time. The Langdon family who lived at Parrocks Lodge – the impressive building that looks at the church from across the main road

Perry Street House, South Chard, in around 1910, the home of Charles Small, whose lace factory was on the opposite side of the road

– were also generous patrons. Parrocks was built in 1801 by John Deane, and later it was home to nine Langdon children, none of whom married. The top storey of the building was demolished in the 1960s and, today, sadly in keeping with the fate of so many fine country houses, has become residential flats.

The vicar there between 1957-76 was Nicholas Francis Domville Coleridge, a descendant of Samuel Taylor Coleridge who was born in 1772 at nearby Ottery St Mary in Devon, where his father was the vicar and master of the King's School. As recently as 2000 St John's became reunited with its original mother church of St Mary's in Chard when the Chard team was formed.

Inside, St John's is a simple enough building but there is one memorial that is worth a second look, especially to local footballers. It is to Charles Edward Small, the owner of the Perry Street Lace Works whom we met in Chapter One. He was a keen devotee of sport in general and cricket and football in particular, and he was the man who started the Perry Street and District Football League. Unusually, for a junior league, it extends into three counties – Somerset, Devon and Dorset.

Small was a man of much substance and, in the manner of such men, was on the Chard School of Governors, the Chard RDC, a chairman of Chard Parish Council, and also a school manager. He wed late in life – in his early forties – marrying Miss Elsie Dening, the daughter of Samuel

Charles Small, owner of Perry Street Lace Works, seen here around 1915, was the 'father' of the Perry Street & District Football League.

Henry Dening, a member of the engineering family that had its factory at Crimchard in Chard. He lived to see the league well-established, but died aged forty-five on 2 February 1919, a victim of the world-wide influenza epidemic. All the factories in Chard closed at the hour of his internment.

The first known church here was a fourteenth-century chapel of ease dedicated to St Margaret in St Margaret's Lane, South Chard. It is obviously one of South Chard's oldest buildings having been a private house at the time of the Commonwealth when a Mr Deane, a member of an old Tatworth family, lived there. When it was renovated in 1895 there was much alteration made inside and the ceiling replaced. At that time it was found that the walls were three feet thick in places. Less than twenty years later it was found to be unsafe and fell into a state of

Crimchard, Chard, c. 1912. Originally a village in its own right, it became swallowed up by its much larger neighbour. Although many of the cottages are still there, much of the thatch has been replaced.

Chard Junction railway station shortly before its closure to passengers in 1962.

disuse. During the Second World War however, it was press-ganged into use as a classroom for evacuated children. Today it is in private hands.

The building of the Baptist chapel at South Chard began in April 1909 when five stones were laid, one by each of the three deacons, one by the pastor, Mr Thomas Dare, and one by the oldest member of the congregation present, during a ceremony to mark the start of the work which cost around £650. The Full Gospel church arrived in South Chard when an old barn at Manor House was converted and officially opened on 17 March 1956 by Miss M. Stephens of Axmouth.

Tatworth's village hall was built as a war memorial at Dykes Hill at a cost of around £5,000, the money being raised from dances, whist drives, flower shows and other social activities after a public meeting in 1945. In 1951 Sister Ethem, of Parrocks, left a legacy of about £2,000 and, after Messrs J.C. Small & Tidmus Ltd, the local net manufacturers, gave the land, the hall was officially opened in November 1953.

For such small places, Perry Street and Chard Junction had and still have, more than their fair share of industry. Between the two places, the butter factory, part of the Wilts United Dairy empire, attracted international attention in 1958 when it produced a then-world record 104 tons of butter in a single day – even the Russian press carried the story. To put it in its proper perspective, 104 tons of butter is equal to

37

Chard Road Hotel, Chard Junction, c. 1904.

931,840 quarter-pound packs. And even Tesco would not turn its nose up at that! In fact 100 tons of butter was said to be enough to supply 3 million people with a day's requirement at the time.

The factory had broken its own record of eighty-six tons. No other butter-making factory had ever exceeded fifty tons in a day, although that figure had been reached in New Zealand. Chard Junction's output, therefore, in terms of a single day's figure, had doubled that of any other factory in the world.

When the shift began their record bid at midnight on 10 June that year, five gigantic rotary churns moved into action, one more than the number when the previous eighty-six-ton record was achieved in 1957. By two o'clock on Wednesday afternoon the old record passed and two hours later the 100-ton mark was reached.

To make 100 tons of butter, Wilts United needed 40,000 gallons of cream which took 600,000 gallons of milk from 200,000 cows to produce. The 100,000 gallons of water needed was taken from the River Axe which flows beside the factory.

In charge of the record bid was the foreman Harold Summers, a Winsham man, who was awarded the BEM in 1950 for his part in that year's record of sixty four tons. As *Pulman's Weekly News*, a popular local paper, proudly claimed, 'And that, mark you, not from an industrial major city, but from the heart of the countryside – from a spick and span building standing at the junction of the counties of Somerset, Dorset and Devon with the River Axe flowing placidly beside it.'

The factory also attracted the attention of the Luftwaffe on 23 October 1942, when, just after four o'clock, a bomber, the pilot probably thinking he was attacking a key industrial site, dropped four bombs. They were dropped from too low an altitude and bounced over the target, which escaped any serious damage but one person, a Mr Hodge from Chardstock, was killed and nearly thirty injured. Windows in Tatworth were broken by the blast – as far as the Co-op shop over half a mile away.

Two miles north of Tatworth, along the line of the Fosse Way, is the turning for Winsham where the Congregational church was founded in 1662 when the vicar of the parish, the Revd William Ball was deprived of the living for refusing to conform with the Act of Uniformity. He founded an independent congregation in the village which he spiritually led until his death in 1670. When the Toleration Act came into force the Winsham congregation appointed as their minister the Revd S. Bolster who obtained a house and equipped it for services in 1703. For a spell ministers from Ilminster, Chard, Crewkerne, and even as far away as Colyton, took the services. In 1760, however, Winsham again had its

Everyone thinks that the summers were always better in the 'good old days'. Some of the winters were colder as well, as evidenced here in this 1902 picture when Chard Reservoir was frozen over. The ice was thick enough to allow sheep roasting and also to take the weight of dozens of people.

own minister and it was during his time there that a new chapel was built to accommodate the increasing number of worshippers. This chapel was replaced in 1810 by the larger chapel which is still in use today in Fore Street. A school room was added in 1863. The old village school in Church Street, built in 1887, has moved to the other side of the road, the original building now being used as the village hall.

Winsham has an unusual nursery. Tucked away in Broadenham Lane, almost as if it did not want to be found, the Kingsfield Conservation Nursery run by local man Geoff Peacock, sells British wild flowers, shrubs and trees. There is nothing quite like the names of our wild flowers, certainly not those of the garden varieties. Geoff will sell you seeds of the squared-stalked St John's wort, the mouse-eared hawkweed, the nettle-leafed bell flower, the hairy St John's wort, the houndstongue, the greater stitchwort and a host of other flowers including those probably more familiar to us all. For a matter of just a few pence you can go away clutching an eight-inch Poplar lombardy but – take heed – it will not stay eight inches high for long. Sadly the old elm tree is no longer on the list.

Roughly south-west of Winsham, but on the Dorset bank of the River Axe which forms the Somerset-Dorset boundary at that point, Forde Abbey is strictly outside this story. However, most people subconsciously think it is in Winsham and we feel it is too important a place locally to leave it out altogether.

Church Street, Winsham, in around 1905.

Fore Street, Winsham, c. 1904. In fact, Church Street, not Fore Street, is Winsham's main thoroughfare.

The rich water meadows at Forde were given to the Cistercian order in 1138 by Adelicia, the sister of Richard de Redvers, Baron of Okehampton, in exchange for the barren ground at Brightley on Dartmoor where an abbey had existed for a short spell. The last abbot was Thomas Chard who was born at Awliscombe near Honiton. He was educated at St Bernard's College at Oxford. In 1521 he became the last abbot of Forde. Happily, although Forde was taken from the monks, it was never destroyed and, after the Dissolution of 1539, Henry VIII granted Forde Abbey to Richard Pollard on a twenty-one-year lease at a rent of £49 6s 6d. During the next 100 years the abbey was to change hands many times: Pollard's son sold the property to Sir Amis Poulett of Hinton St George who sold it to William Rosewell, Queen Elizabeth's Solicitor-General. His son, another William, sold it to Edmund Prideaux, a staunch Parliamentarian during the Civil War when he held the post of Attorney-General to Oliver Cromwell and he was the first man to organize a regular weekly delivery of letters to all parts of the country. The profit from his postal services and other posts brought in some £22,000 a year – a massive sum for the times.

High above Winsham, on the hills overlooking Chard from the east, a magnificent row of beech trees line the old A30 coach road that runs along the ridge to Crewkerne and beyond. Halfway along that road is

Windwhistle Inn on the A30 trunk road above Cricket St Thomas. Once said to be the haunt of both highwaymen and smugglers, this popular inn is still there and still flanked by one of the most attractive rows of beech trees in the area.

the Windwhistle Inn, once the haunt of smugglers and highwaymen. Reference is made to the inn in 1782 and it is possibly the same building as a Black Horse Inn that stood on the same stretch of road. Just below the southern side of the ridge is Cricket St Thomas and Cricket House, the latter known by millions as the setting for the BBC comedy series *To The Manor Born* featuring Penelope Keith and Peter Bowles. The tiny hamlet takes its name from *cruche*, a Celtic word for hill from which the de Crickets family who lived there in the fourteenth century got their name. Cricket stands beside the Purtington Brook which joins the Axe by Forde Abbey at the spot where the main river forms the Somerset-Devon boundary.

There are references to a manor house here as early as 1313 but the present building dates from the end of the eighteenth century when it was bought by Captain Alexander Hood. It was rebuilt at that time after a disastrous fire, Hood employing Sir John Soane, the well-known architect, to do the work.

Captain Hood had a good career taking part in several engagements with the French, including the Battle of Cape St Vincent (1794), forever known in naval folklore as 'The Glorious 1st of June'. For his part in that battle, Hood, by now a Vice Admiral, was created Baron Bridport of Cricket St Thomas and later became Viscount Bridport. Twice married but childless, he was buried in Cricket St Thomas church in 1814 at the age of eighty-seven. The estate went to his great-nephew Samuel who had married one of Lord Nelson's nieces. It was again sold in 1897 by another Alexander Hood, the great-great-nephew of the first Viscount, who had gone against family tradition by becoming a general. The new owner was the chocolate manufacturer Francis James Fry. It then went through a succession of owners before becoming a Wildlife Park in the 1960s. *To the Manor Born* is not Cricket's only association with television: Noel Edmunds brought his 'Mr Blobby' there as a major attraction for a short spell in the 1990s. Today Cricket House is a hotel complex.

To the north of the Windwhistle Ridge can be found a series of small hamlets that stretch almost as far as Dowlish Wake to the south of Ilminster. The average tourist never sees them, as they are hidden around leafy corners in deep sunken lanes with chert and flint more to the fore than Ham stone. The nearest to Chard is Chaffcombe just off the line of the Chard Canal and the old Taunton-Chard railway branch line.

Here the parish church of St Michael and All Angels stands a little aloof from the rest of the village on which it gazes down through trees of all sorts and sizes, including two handsome Lebanese cedars. Shortly after we visited the church (June 2002) one of the cedar trees, which sloped at an alarming angle, was cut down in the interests of safety. But not the church's safety, the tree leant away from it. However, if it did come down in a storm a lot of gravestones would have been in danger. Among the other trees is an obligatory yew of uncertain age.

Just inside the south porch a sign tells one that The Incorporated Society for Buildings and Churches gave £45 to reseating the church on condition that of the 133 seats, numbers 1-19 were reserved for the poor inhabitants of the village. There are six bells, the fifth dating from the fifteenth century and the tenor, weighing in at 10.5 cwt, is dated 1733. The treble was added as recently as 1970 when the bells were re-hung and given a new framework. The slim tower, restored in the fifteenth century by Sir Amias Poulett, who is said to be buried in the church, is a typical example of the Somerset style and has an attractive little turret in one corner. The whole church was restored in the Early English style around 1859, and contains an unusual guilt reredos which is a memorial to Revd Clurteis Henry Norwood, rector here between 1879-88. There is an Elizabethan paten and a chalice dated 1574. The old rectory lies behind the church and, as was usual for the Victorians, it is close to looking foreboding and is much too grand for such a humble little place.

Humble or not Chaffcombe has some lovely old cottages, especially the Old School House which was not the school, that is now the village hall, but the home of the headmaster who occupied half of the building that stands at right angles to the lane. Beside the School House, a row of cottages running parallel to the lane were once hovels but were rebuilt as farm workers' dwelling places. Both buildings are in stone and are thatched. Instead of following the lane to the church, keep straight on and April Cottage is on the right. This was once part of the old saw mills. The oldest cottages in Chaffcombe are probably Pound Cottage and its neighbour Wisteria Cottage, which date from around 1650-1700.

Climb the hill beyond April Cottage and – Somerset lanes are eccentrically signpost free in many places – follow your nose to Cricket Malherbie and another lovely church, St Mary Magdalene, where there really are bats in the belfry. The swallow that nests in the porch is readily seen, but no one ever sees the bats, whose existence is only known because of their 'calling cards' that need sweeping up before services.

St Mary's is unusual in south-west Somerset in that it has a small spire rather than a tower. This may be due to the fact that it was entirely rebuilt on the site of the old building in around 1865 in memory of Stephen Pitt, a lieutenant in the 82nd Regiment, who died in India in 1865 aged twenty-one. The tiny north transept contains the Squire's Pew, and memorials to Stephen Pitt, from his brother officers, to Charlotte Pitt (died 1903) and to Stephen's father, George, who died seven months after his son. George was a cousin to two British prime ministers; Pitt the Elder, first earl of Chatham and prime minister between 1766-68, and Pitt the Younger, who formed two separate governments between 1783-1801 and 1804-06. In post-war years the estate belonged to Lord Beaverbrook.

Behind the pew the stained-glass window depicts three scenes from Mary Magdalene's life. In the central window she is seen anointing Jesus' feet, on one side Jesus appears after the Resurrection, the other is said to show her listening to Jesus while Martha goes about the housework. This is wrong of course, it is Mary of Bethany and not Mary Magdalen who should be depicted there. On the north wall a large crucifix was the work of Italian prisoners of war who were interned in Cricket Court and worked on the farm during the Second World War. The tracery and windows here are Ham stone but the rest of the building is in an inferior local stone.

Opposite the church, Cricket Court replaced the old manor house just after the Napoleonic wars by Admiral Pitt who, if the story is to be believed, acted as his own architect. In later years the writer Nikolaievich Tolstoy spent some time here and attended church dressed in a frock coat. On one occasion he lit a small fire in the Squire's Pew and smoked out all the parishioners. It is thought that the bats were unmoved.

Lydmarsh is so sparsely inhabited that it hardly warrants the title of hamlet but is does contain Avishayes House, brick-built and seventeenth-century, and given a new facade by James Marwood in 1775. At the same time the large park was created. Lydmarsh may be sparsely inhabited but just outside of Chard it does stretch across the A30 as far as Kingstonwell Farm, which is almost on the Fosse Way where the B3162 crosses it on the way to Winsham. On the A30 once stood the Happy Return public house. Now a private dwelling its name had been usurped by the former Railway Inn in Chard's East Street.

Cudworth and Chillington stand on the northern slopes of Windwhistle Hill looking out towards Dowlish Wake. Chillington, the nearest hamlet to the Fosse Way, which clambers the slopes of Windwhistle Hill (712 feet at that point) is isolated in a steep little valley and there is nothing there apart from a few houses and farms. The same

The Beara, Wambrook, in 1903. This was the home of William Salter Beviss, a well-known Chard solicitor. His son John followed him into the business and spent four years as a POW during the Second World War.

45

might be said for Cudworth (Cutha's homestead) but for the presence of St Michael's church and the moat that once protected a medieval manor house. Parts of this moat can still be seen in a field immediately behind St Michael's church.

The good people of Cudworth have solved the problem of cutting the churchyard grass by selling the keep to a local sheep farmer, which probably accounts for the larger than usual number of doormats just inside the Norman north doorway. This doorway once led into a much smaller church, the nave and chancel being added in the late thirteenth century. The old altar remains as a small chapel at the end of what now serves as an aisle. Behind is what surely has to be a unique, tiny, Norman window behind the original east window. On St Michael's Day, the Summer Solstice, the sun rises directly in line with this window, which might suggest the existence of a pagan place of worship in earlier days.

Near a filled-in south doorway is a handsome, if well worn, Jacobean pulpit with a thirteenth-century font in front of it. The older church walls are plastered but those in the chancel are made from large flint stones or rubble, although Ham stone has been used in the windows and doors. The windows come from three separate periods; Early English on the north aisle, lovely Decorated windows in the chancel and, equally lovely, Perpendicular in the west window. The roof above the nave is medieval but restored in 1904 when the barrel-vaulted roof in the chancel was added. All in all a simple little church with much to see and admire.

Outside, before going across the churchyard to see the moat and the flint-built Knights House Farm, note the bellcote with two bells, one dated 1607, the other 1678 and by that famous bell founder Thomas Purdue.

West of Chard, on the other side of the high arm of the Blackdown Hills that runs all the way from Brown Down to Tytherleigh just over the county boundary with Devonshire on the Axminster road lies Wambrook. It is tucked into in a narrow valley near the headwaters of the Kit Brook that runs away below Chardstock to join the Axe a few yards above Broom Crossing at Chilson where Somerset's most southerly inhabitants live. Here, and at neighbouring Cotley, it is easy to become lost among the narrow, twisting lanes but well worth that risk to visit St Mary's little church where the treasures include a gallery for the bell-ringers and some sixteenth-century bench-ends. The church stands in particularly attractive countryside, all trees and thatch, and if you fancy some sustenance before heading on towards Buckland St Mary and Bishopswood, where better than the New Inn at Cotley where Dennetts Farm – next to the inn – is of an uncertain age.

Above Wambrook and on the other side of the main A30 road, Combe St Nicholas is said to have had a church since 970 when Queen Aelfthryth founded one there. She was the second wife of King Edgar and is best known for the murder of her stepson, Edward the Martyr at Corfe Castle in 979, thus clearing the way for her own son Ethelred the Unready (979-1016) to become King. The present church took the place of a later Norman building in 1239 and was dedicated to St Nicholas, but there was considerable work and enlargement in the fifteenth century when north and south aisles, the nave and the rood screen were added. At the same time two external turrets were added and it is possible that the tower was also increased to its present sixty-foot height at the same time. Inside the five-bayed, Ham stone arcade is particularly attractive and the ancient sandstone, probably pre-Conquest, font is also well worth a second glance. The top is worn – by knife sharpening according to local tradition. There is a peal of six bells, the heaviest being the tenor which weighs in at 14cwt, and dated 1613 it bears the inscription 'Draw near to God'.

The Wadeford branch of Chard Industrial & Provident Society Limited seen here around 1910.

The West Country in general, and Devonshire in particular, is famous for its magnificent chancel screens and the screen at St Nicholas's is well up to those high standards. Dating from 1470s, Combe's no longer carries the Holy Rood, St John the Evangelist and the Virgin Mary; they would have vanished during the Reformation. A later desecrator, one Oliver Cromwell, also 'removed' Thomas Greenfield from the living and he was thought to have died in prison in London. Now we know that he returned to Combe after the Restoration in 1660 and died there eleven years later.

Of interest to local footballers will be a brass plaque on the tower screen which reads:

> *To the Glory of God and in Memory of Frederick Henry Wheaton. Born December 2nd 1885, died February 12th 1938. For 22 years schoolmaster of this parish and associated with the administration of the Perry Street and District Football League since 1903. A tribute to his character and service, this screen was erected by his many friends in 1938.*

Henry Wheaton was secretary of the Perry Street & District Football League, taking office just after the First World War until his death at the age of fifty-three. He played for Perry Street Works until he moved to Combe to become a much-loved headmaster at the local school for twenty-two years.

Lying beneath Combe and much smaller, Wadeford's most interesting feature has to be Nimmer Mills, once one of several corn mills on the River Isle between Chard and Ilminster. Few, if any, working water mills other than show features remain today, hundreds having fallen into disuse in the past fifty or sixty years. Nimmer, however, got out of the milling 'rat race' as far back as around 1810 when James Coates, with his associates, members of the McLennan family, started manufacturing toilet brushes at Nimmer. They also owned the London Brush Works at the foot of Castle Hill in Axminster. Contact between the two mills was maintained by donkey transport with a daily exchange of loads at Tytherleigh between a cart from Nimmer and one from Axminster. William Ward, grandson of the original William Ward, who was the driver of the donkey cart, was still working as a general factotum in 1960 when he told *Pulman's Weekly News* that the donkey, which was very old when it was finally pensioned off, was kept in the orchard at Nimmer.

The village green at Combe St Nicholas, c. 1905. The lamp standard on the right commemorates Queen Victoria's Diamond Jubilee of 1897.

The Coates connection continued until 1940 when a Mr Alec Simpson's brush-making factory in London was destroyed during the Blitz. He moved down to Nimmer, bought out the Coates family and set up two companies there: A. Simpson (Brushes) Ltd mostly made shaving brushes, and Coates Brushes Ltd turned out the remainder of the toilet-brush range; hair brushes, nail brushes, etc. The brushes were not mass-produced but turned out to a high standard by hand, quite a few being made by out-workers who were called on daily at their homes. Simpson's exported all over the world with their shaving brushes, costing as much as £25-£30 – a considerable sum at the time – being made especially for the North American market. Badger hair was always used for the shaving brushes and ten badgers were needed to provide one pound of hair, which cost £20 in the middle of the twentieth century. A speciality at that time were shaving brushes with handles made from ivory.

Nimmer Mills is currently being restored by Chris Black who very kindly took us on a conducted tour of the building, which still retains its massive water wheel. He has a tough job on hand as the place has been sadly neglected and there is a lot to be done before Chris realizes his ambition of starting a textile craft centre there. At present he has to share it with the swallows in the summer and, probably, a barn owl or two. He also intends to have a small museum dedicated to the brush manufacturing business. A start has been made in that direction – the renovation work is constantly unearthing samples of brushes and the tools with which they were made.

Close by, Pudleigh cloth mills was the last of the Chard cloth mills, ceasing trade in the late nineteenth century after being in production since 1780 when the Brown family set up business there and made stout cloth to high standards. Partly demolished, it became a fish farm and today there is hardly any trace of the old buildings.

Buckland St Mary, to the north-west of Chard high up in the Blackdown Hills (and just off the line of the busy A303 trunk road before it drops down to the new Ilminster bypass), is said to get it name from it being land granted by the Saxon kings to their nobles. It is a village of mostly flint but there is some Ham stone, especially in the parish church of St Mary the Virgin, a modern building that was built in 1853-63 on the site of a previous building. There was certainly a church here in Norman days, and it is almost as certain that one would have superseded a Saxon building. The only remains of the Norman church are said to be the cross on the war memorial in the churchyard. The earliest known rector was Robertus (1318).

Inside St Mary's it is dark and gloomy, and the unusual dark floral tiles covering the walls around the altar do not help. But that is a price most visitors are happy to pay for the superb stained-glass, including the west window which is a based on the famous window at Fairford in Gloucestershire. A clerestory might have helped to do away with the gloom, but the presence of twelve carved figures high on the walls above the nave make that impossible. The figures are those of the twelve Apostles, each with their name below. The reredos shows Christ being taken down from the Cross by the Virgin Mary and two angels with two more angels in the panel on either side. For such a small church there are two aisles with attractive slim pillars.

Most of the work was done in flint with some Ham stone by a Mr Davis of Taunton who employed local workmen, including Mr Gahagen, a sculptor, whose head along with that of his wife, are said to be those carved outside, below the scrolls on the window to the left of the south door.

The cost of building the new church was largely met by the rector, Revd John Edwin Lance, whose considerable financial interests in France had been in jeopardy when they were impounded during the

February Revolution of 1848 when Napoleon's nephew seized power and later (1852) ruled as Napoleon III. Lance's money was safe, however, and his generosity was so great that the village was asked to find only £500 towards the building costs of the church. Mrs Madelina Lance is remembered in the church by a monument on which, unusually so, she is depicted as breaking free from her tomb.

The surprisingly large rectory on the hill above the village was built by Revd Lance for himself. He obviously went in for his creature comforts; his rectory contained a library and a decent cellar as well as nine bedrooms and plenty of accommodation for the staff which included a butler in charge of a workforce of around a dozen others.

Opposite the church, the village school is also unusually large for such a small place but modern needs have even seen the addition of a new and separate classroom. In the wall of the school playground a roofed pump supplied the village with its water. The pump has been replaced by a tap, and the stone seating on either side is useful for the modern generation who use it as a bus stop.

There is little to detain one in Buckland St Mary, especially as the village pub, the Lamb and Flag, has been closed. A former dwelling place, it became an inn as far back as 1837. Nowadays it is only remembered

A squire-like person poses outside the Eagle Tavern at Buckland St Mary around 1906. One hopes he bought the two workers a drink!

in the names of two houses, Lamb House and Flag House, on the site of the old inn. The Castle Inn, on the edge of Dommett Moor on the Taunton Road a mile outside the village, has also closed, but the Eagle Tavern, a much more modern building, is still open. It dates from the same time as the Lamb & Flag but benefits from the passing trade on the busy A303. This is indeed the high Blackdowns, the Castle Inn and Dommett Moor standing at just below the 900-foot (272m).

Buckland St Mary has been encapsulated for all time by Patricia Wendors in her novel *Larksleeve*, among others.

Below Buckland St Mary, Bishopswood lies on the western slopes of the River Yarty a mile or so below its source at Blackwater (below the old Castle Inn) and some two miles above Marsh where the river enters Devon on its way to join the Axe at Axminster. Keates Mill on the Yarty was a working mill down until the 1930s. Towards the top of the hamlet the chapel is dated 1874. The post office stores has gone but the seventeenth-century New Inn, renamed the Candlelight Inn around the 1970s, is still there. The hamlet is a mixture of old and attractive flint and some equally attractive colour-washed new buildings.

Climb over Brown Down to the west of Bishopswood to Churchinford, where the York Inn lost its skittle alley through fire in 2001. This was a pity, the team that played in the Colyton Skittle League, one of the strongest leagues in Devon, picked up six titles, finished second twice, third six times, fourth once and fifth four times in nineteen years before age caught up with it. Nothing odd about the Somerset village playing in a Devon skittle league, the village's very popular cricket team play in the Devon Cricket League. Almost in Devon, Churchstanton is the church without a village. That church, dedicated to SS Peter and Paul stands in a field with only farm houses for its neighbours. The oldest part of the church is thought to be the west tower which probably dates from around the end of the twelfth century. Otherwise most the building is from the Perpendicular period. Despite its isolated position there is much to see in this church, especially the arcade to the south aisle and the gallery which was constructed out of the bench ends the thought to have been replaced in 1830 by the almost overpowering box pews. Corporal James Doble of the Coldstream Guards, is remembered on the west wall for his bravery and death at the Battle of Inkerman (1854) in the Crimean War.

THREE

Crewkerne

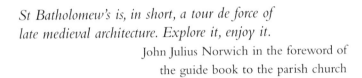

*St Batholomew's is, in short, a tour de force of
late medieval architecture. Explore it, enjoy it.*
John Julius Norwich in the foreword of
the guide book to the parish church

Unlike Chard, Crewkerne is mostly Ham stone, especially the parish
church of St Bartholomew, much of which is fifteenth century, but on
the site of a church that existed there in the reign of King Alfred. It is an
ancient town, having its own mint before the Conquest. George Pulman
tells us that Collison claims that its name stems from the Anglo-Saxon
cruce or cross and *earne*, a cottage. Today most people agree with the
cottage but think that *cruche* is Celtic and means a sheltered place. If so
this adds strength to Crewkerne's claim to antiquity.

But it seems to have been a late developer, the celebrated itinerant
Leland saying of the place around 1540;

> *Crokehorn is sette under rootes of a hille. Ther I saw nothing very notable.
> Yet ther ys a praty crosse environed with smaul pillars a praty toune house
> yn the market place.*

John Leland was commissioned by Henry VIII (1509-47) to make a
survey and record the antiquities of the Realm, a sort of up-market
Domesday we suppose, and he included the ancient buildings that he
passed, events connected with the area he was passing through, and also
the nature and character of the countryside. Although his exact route
through Somerset is not known, a ramblers' walk, the Leland Trail, runs
the twenty-eight miles from the border of Wiltshire to end at Ham Hill
a few miles east of Crewkerne.

East Street, Crewkerne, c. 1908, seen from the Market Square.

Agriculture would have been the main occupation when Leland passed through Crewkerne, but the cloth industry began to take over and, by the eighteenth century, the production of sail cloth had become important and this, along with the production of serges for the East India Company, saw a considerable expansion in the size of the town.

Crewkerne's wealth once lay in the weaving industry, the arrival of the railway in 1860 giving the town a boost. The station is actually in Misterton, Crewkerne's nearest neighbour, and for years the landlords of the Red Lion and the George in Crewkerne would play a game of dominoes to see which one of them would operate the coach for the coming year. That coach was known as the 'sixpenny coach', the fare from the station to the town.

A one-mile stretch of the Southern Railway Waterloo-Exeter main line between Crewkerne and Sutton Bingham saw the arrival of the first 300-foot lengths of rail to be used in the country in 1955. They were welded on the spot and fixed on eight-inch concrete sleepers against the normal five-inch wooden ones, thus providing an unbroken stretch of track laid on a specially designed base. From then onwards the heavy trains hurtled over them at speeds of eighty miles an hour without a sound or a rock or a roll.

Once installed the rails were inspected twice every Friday by Mr Brown, the chief ganger for that part of the line, who took their temperatures. If the rails were too hot, 100 degrees or, in railway jargon, blood heat, he would come back the following day to make sure they had returned to normal.

Mr Brown was born at Misterton in 1892 and joined the railway company in 1912. He retired in 1958 after forty-six years service. During his last nine years his four-man gang won the £14-pound prize for the best-kept track length on that line six times.

The gatekeeper's cottage at the crossing at Hewish, between Crewkerne and Wayford, drew its water from an old well which caved in during 1958. After that the gatekeeper, Bill Poole, received his water daily in churns by the 2.40 p.m. train from Yeovil. Bill was unhappy about it, he only got two five-gallon churns for three grown-ups, and there was no 2.40 train on Sundays when they went without water. And the churns were far from clean, Bill being recorded as pointing out, 'They would not supply in milk in churns that were rusty.' He was to go without water for some time. His cottage was in Chard Rural Council's area and they claimed they could not supply him. Crewkerne Council were also approached and they said they would not supply him. He went

Church Street, Crewkerne, at its junction with Market Street and Market Square, c. 1900. The drinking tap and horse trough is no longer there, a traffic island complete with flower beds having taken its place when the road became part of a one-way system.

Crewkerne's famous Pride of the West Band c. 1912. It was a poor outdoor function that did not have the band on parade. Its speciality was playing before and during the interval at all Crewkerne's big football matches.

to the National Union of railwaymen, but eighteen months later the cottage was still dry.

Twenty-eight years before the railway arrived Crewkerne was lit by gas for the first time. The original gas works were on the slopes to the east of the town but moved to a new home near Viney Bridge in 1854. But the works did not supply the whole town, at least two factories making their own gas on their premises.

Much of the town's industry during the later Victorian years was busy producing canvass and webbing, Arthur Hart & Son in Station Road being the largest webbing manufacturers in the West Country and supplying it for the reins and girths for racehorses among other things. Belts for military uniforms, especially during the First World War, was another speciality. There were other webbing mills in South Street.

George Rigby Pulman was born just over the border in Axminster's Lyme Street on 21 February 1819. The son of a Colyton blacksmith, he spent thirty of his almost sixty-one years in Crewkerne. Some might argue that his best claim to fame stems from the fact that, among many other books, he was the author of *Pulman's Book of the Axe*, a half piscatorial and half historical (and generally truthful) story of the river that, after rising in Dorset in the hills above Beaminster, runs through the extreme southern part of our story before escaping into the sea near Seaton. Widely quoted, a first edition fetches over a thousand pounds on the rare occasion that one come up for sale.

Others might claim that the newspaper he founded in 1857, *Pulman's Weekly News*, is better known, it has certainly been read by more people. That paper once covered an area bounded by Bridport, Yeovil, Taunton, Honiton and Sidmouth. It is still published today, indeed appropriately so in Axminster hardly more than a stone's throw from the house in which Pulman was born. Today it tends to cover the Axe Valley and the Honiton area. Although both George and his wife Jane are buried at Axminster, his name lives on in Crewkerne as Pulman Lane which is now buried under a car park.

Staying with the *Pulman's* connection, staff reporter Eric Hopkins, later editor, once wrote of an interesting find made by Dr McCell, the town's medical officer, before he moved from Orchard Cottage. In an old built-in wall safe a George III shilling, a Victorian sixpence and notebook crumbling with age were found. The book contained a list of the members between 1850-1900 of the Blues Friendly Society, one of two such societies in the town who met at the Royal Oak in Hermitage Street. The other Society, The Reds, had their HQ at the Swan.

At Whitsuntide both societies held their annual festival combining for what was known as the 'Club Walk'. With 'Boxer' Bennett and Thomas

The West Somerset Shirt Factory, Crewkerne, were always in the thick of the town's social life; members of the staff are seen here performing at a concert between the wars. Their star turn was undoubtedly their large walking entry at Crewkerne carnivals, and in 1935 over 100 employees took part in the carnival for King George V's Silver Jubilee. They were dressed in red, white and blue and were headed by their own jazz band.

Churchill as standard bearers. Members, carrying either a large red or a blue pole, six foot high and mounted with a large brass ornament, paraded through the town headed by the local Pride of the West band. After a service at St Bartholomew's parish church and a dinner at their headquarters, the men were joined by their families and all went off to Parsonage Field for sports. In the evening there was dancing on the green and, judging from an entry at the back of the old notebook, quite an amount of beer was consumed. A tradition was that new potatoes were always on the menu for the dinner, and to make sure of this members always grew their own.

Although Crewkerne was never part of the main stream of the Civil War, Hinton St George was on its doorstep. This was the home of Lord Poulett who raised a regiment of foot at his own expense, many of his men coming from Crewkerne to join him in harrassing the Somerset and Devon borders. One of their moments came when he marched his men to Musbury where Lady Drake's Ashe House home was being guarded by a troop of Parliamentarian soldiers from Lyme Regis. The noble lord burnt Ashe House to the ground, her ladyship escaping barefoot and half naked to Lyme. A few years later her daughter gave birth to John Churchill at rebuilt Ashe. Churchill, who would one day become the Duke of Marlborough, may have been on the James II's side when he

By the 1930s another kind of horsepower was taking over the Crewkerne streets and, although the cars did not need stables, they certainly needed parking spaces, as evidenced here in Market Square. Cars still park there, if off the road now, and a roundabout and non-priority pedestrian crossing has appeared.

The Morris Minors from the picture opposite. Taken at the same time, this one looks into East Street where, in the background, a bus heads for Yeovil.

came to Somerset chasing the Duke of Monmouth's army, but he deserted him in 1688 and joined William of Orange who spent the night of 25 November in Crewkerne on his way to London from Torbay.

But first the Bloody Assizes came to Somerset and ten men were hung, drawn and quartered in Crewkerne after the Duke of Monmouth's defeat at Sedgemoor. George Pulman does not say they were Crewkernians but lists them as John Spore, Roger Burnell, William Pether, James Every, Robert Hill, Nicholas Adams, Richard Stephens, Robert Halswell, John Bussell and William Lashley. One local man who did suffer was Captain Madders, the constable of Crewkerne, who was executed at Lyme Regis for his part in the rebellion.

Another celebrity said to have visited the town is Dick Turpin, legend having him staying at the Green Dragon in Market Square, one of four inns once owned by Crewkerne Grammar School; the others included the Bell and the White Hart. Queen Anne's Building was built on the site of the Green Dragon in 1885 while the nearby George Hotel existed as early as 1541 and by 1735 there were twenty-two licensed houses in the town and thirty-five by 1751. Just outside the town the Blue Ball at Roundham dates from 1770 before when it was the Bottle. Today it is the Travellers Rest.

John Combe, vicar at St Bartholemew's church from 1472, is credited with the founding of Crewkerne Grammar School. He left Crewkerne for Exeter in 1486 but he died in 1499, after giving some land to endow a free grammar school and master in the town. If the school was not continued the monies from the land had to be spent on repairing the roads of the town. Probably the most famous of the pupils at Crewkerne was Sir Thomas Hardy, Nelson's captain who is remembered in a mural in the town car park. Hardy became First Sea Lord in 1830. Another famous Crewkernian was Ralph Reader (1903-82) who made his name as innovator of the Boy Scouts Gang Shows. He was born in 1903 in the Post Horn Café in Court Barton. The grammar school became Wadham Comprehensive School in 1972.

Roundham, outside the town on the A30 to the west, and just before that road climbs over Windwhistle Hill, once featured prominently in Crewkerne's sporting life, a race course flourishing there between 1906-22 and for many years the area's big football matches were played on the race course there rather than in the town itself. The biggest was the Crewkerne Hospital Cup final, the first amateur knock-out competition in an area that stretches from Yeovil to Honiton and south to Bridport. It was started in 1910 when Mr George Dyson of Merriott donated the handsome trophy. The first final, between Petters United and Boden from Chard, raised £45 from the three games needed before Petters won 2-1. Gates of 2,000 were not uncommon in the finals held there. When the race course was closed just after the First World War the grandstand was bought by Axminster Town football club and taken to their ground at Sector in that town where it served for another fifty or so years.

Crewkerne obtained its hospital after a public meeting in the Town Hall in 1866 after an offer of a building in South Street by Robert Bird, a generous benefactor of the town who employed nearly 200 workers in his webbing factory in South Street where one of the buildings was to become the new hospital. The speed with which the hospital was completed, it opened eight months later in 1867, contrasted sharply with the eight years of discussions needed before work on an extension to Crewkerne's new hospital's outpatients department even started. A new hospital was opened in Gas Lane in 1904 at a cost of £5,300; it was taken over by the NHS in 1948.

St Bartholomew's church stands just back from the town centre and at the end of an attractive cul-de-sac which, many would claim,

The People's Picture Palace, Market Square, Crewkerne, c. 1920. Formerly known as the Victoria Hall, the original building was constructed as a market house in 1730.

contains some of the town's better buildings. Like so many of Somerset's churches it is in the Perpendicular style and its size, if not its beauty, is an indication of the wealth that the woollen trade had brought to the town by the late fifteenth century. The west front is particularly handsome, Dr Freeman claiming it is 'one of the finest belonging to any parish church in England', although the good people of Colyton might take issue on that point. It is indeed a wonderful church standing on the site of a Saxon building founded there during the reign of Alfred the Great. The oldest part of the present building, however, are to be found in the piers and supports of the central crossing tower which date from the thirteenth century. In the fifteenth and sixteenth century St Bartholomew's was virtually rebuilt in the lovely Perpendicular style which is made even more attractive by the use of the stone from nearby Ham Hill.

Not even the word magnificent does justice to that west front and its lovely, seven-light window, both exceptional for a town of this size. The window stands above an attractively carved doorway, inside which is the end of the nave. But all the twenty-four windows here are superb, those in the north and south aisles probably the best after the west window. It

61

is the six-light size of these windows, rather than the clerestory itself, that gives the nave and its two wide aisles their light and cheerful appearance.

Like so many of our churches, St Bartholomew's fell into the hands of the Victorian restorers. Happily, at Crewkerne, the work was done by the eminent Diocesan architect Mr J.D. Sedding, who not only had a love of beautiful churches but he was especially enamoured with the Perpendicular style and, if possible, St Bartholomew's was much improved by him.

Inside one is immediately struck by the beauty of the nave and its arcades. The position of the central crossing tower means that the nave is fairly short which is a pity. But that is more than made up for by the tower and its buttresses and the chancel beyond, including a finely carved reredos depicting the Last Supper, made of Ham stone and a gift of Miss Hussey in 1903. This is a church in which one could and should spend a morning both wandering around inside and sitting outside in the sunshine and taking in the surrounding houses, easily the best part of the town.

Almost without exception, England's memorials to the dead of two wars feature prominently in the towns and villages. One exception, however, is at Crewkerne's where the war memorial was erected in 1921 in the middle of the half-built Severalls council estate and a tree, each with a lead name-plate bearing the name of one of the fallen, was

First World War casualties about to leave Crewkerne station for the local hospital.

planted there for every Crewkerne man who made the supreme sacricfice during the First World War. Some of the lead plate can be seen in Crewkerne's museum.

Robert Gibbs borrowed £500 from a relative in 1862 to set himself up as an agricultural agent using his house in South Street as an office. From there he toured the local markets selling ploughs, harrows, cultivators and sowing machines. By 1875 he had prospered enough to move to bigger premises in Oxen Road where his only son John joined him. They built workshops there and employed four men in repairing machinery. Robert died in 1893, but the business did not flourish under John, and a Mr Abbott of Yeovil, an uncle, put £1,000 into the business and appointed John's son, Hubert Gibbs, to take charge. Hubert was a forceful character and by 1908 he had paid back that £1,000 and went into an equal partnership with his father.

Hubert junior was an inventor as well as a business man. In 1905 his first patent was for a new swathe-turner which he sold to Nicholsons of Newark from whom he received royalties for fourteen years. In 1960 he said, 'It was not a lot of money, but it helped.' But it was in 1916 that the manufacturing side of the business really took off, the patenting of a hay-loader enabling him to secure premises in East Street where seventeen men were employed in its manufacture. Later, labour problems arose and Hubert decided that the interests of his firm would be best served if he closed the factory and sold the patent to Bamford of Uttoxeter who made the most of the opportunity, Hubert's hay loader becoming world famous. At the Royal Show at Cardiff he was awarded the Royal Agricultural Society's silver medal, the highest award for an agricultural machine invention which secured the financial position of the firm.

John died in 1917 at the age of sixty-five, Hubert buying his father's shares and became sole proprietor of a flourishing concern. He next invented a machine for marking white lines in roads, these were manufactured in Crewkerne and distributed by Clare's of Liverpool. These were sold all over the world, as were tennis-court markers and a another hay loader, the latter being also sold to Bamfords in 1944.

It was in 1920 that Hubert sold his first tractor to George Willy of South Petherton. In 1936 the business had grown to such an extent that a new tractor shed was erected in Oxen Road and more premises were obtained at Barn Street and Tower Hill,

When Hubert retired in 1949 his two sons, Jack and Bernard, then took over the business, which was renamed as J. & B. Gibbs and Sons, and by 1954 it was turned into a limited company with a modest capital of £20,000. Business had flourished to such an extent by 1957 that the old Crewkerne Brewery at Broadshard was purchased and all the previous offices and workshops were gathered together under one roof covering an area of 15,000 square feet. Sadly, at the turn of the century, the family sold their interests and the Broadshard premises were sold.

Crewkerne was the birthplace of the firm that perfected probably the world's most well known vacuum cleaner – the Henry. Now known as Numatic International the firm began life in Crewkerne in 1969 when it employed six people in a building just about big enough to house the average family car.

The first cleaners were made out of a combination of oil drums and components that were readily available, such as suitcase handles, furniture castors and domestic washing-up bowls. They were all assembled in such a way as to provide a simple, reliable workhorse for commercial and industrial use. By 1971 output had become too large for such tiny premises and a move was made to a water mill in Yeovil where, when the river flooded, the factory was often under two inches of water. This may have been the catalyst that started the production of wet pick-up machines. It was in Yeovil that the first serious commercial vacuum cleaner was developed, the NV-2, followed very closely by the NV-250. Both were all-steel machines and the majority of them are still working today over thirty years later. And Numatic International proudly claims that it can still produce parts and replacements for all the vacuum cleaners that it has ever produced.

Moving into the cleaning industry, the production of floor polishers and wet and dry cleaners meant the firm had again outgrown its premises and a move was made to Beaminster where Numatic International would stay for twenty years. It was there that the Henry vacuum cleaner was born. It became so famous world-wide that another move had to be made, this time to premises in Chard's industrial estate where over 500 people are employed. So much has the firm increased that parts of the factory are working twenty-four hours a day to produce around 3,000 products daily and subsidiaries have been opened in France and South Africa.

The famous Henry cleaner now produced in Chard by Numatic International, who started out in life in Crewkerne and now export their considerable range of products to over 100 countries.

The post has not always had a happy time in Crewkerne, especially when Thomas Hutchings was the 'post' (master) there in 1622. At that time postmasters throughout the country had many serious grievances, mainly about their remuneration. Thomas emerged as their champion when he collected signatures to a petition which he sent direct to the King (James I) who took the matter seriously enough to appoint a Privy Council Committee to investigate. It sat on 7 December that year and in time reported back that many of the posts were not receiving all the wages due to them, much of it being siphoned off by the Paymaster whose salary was only five shillings a year – in contrast his clerk received 20 marks, which is about £13.

The King accepted that the posts had a justified grievance but Thomas Hutchings was still not happy, especially as Lord Stanhope (the Postmaster General) now wanted to charge him two pounds for sending him and all the other posts a copy of the rules necessary for the carrying out of his duties. He continued badgering authority to such an extent that he was clapped in gaol and Crewkerne was left without a postmaster. His offence was that he petitioned the Secretary of State to 'inform the King of their extreme distress for want of money, their wages being two and a half years in arrears, and they have to provide monies for His Majesty's service.'

He was set free after a somewhat grovelling apology and agreed not to waste his superiors time again nor to raise the matter on pain of being put straight back in gaol without as much as a trial. When he returned to Crewkerne he found that Lord Stanhope had appointed a postmaster in his place and was only reinstalled after an appeal to the Board.

Crewkerne's reputation for awkward postmasters would continue. Later, when the mail for Axminster and East Devon was supposed to be 'sorted'

The Durnovarian coach outside Sparrow's Livery Stables in Church Street, Crewkerne, c. 1900. Who owned the coach is not known but Durnovaria was the Roman name for Dorchester which might suggest it is an outing from that town or that there was regular service between the towns.

at the town and forwarded daily to Axminster by a man on horseback, Crewkerne's postmaster at the time had to pay for the man and the horse. This he refused to do so and forced the Axminster postmaster to send a man to collect the mail. This practice continued until road improvements between Salisbury and the West Country enabled the mail to travel westward from the Wiltshire town via Dorchester, Bridport and Axminster leaving Crewkerne still receiving its mail from Salisbury by a post boy on horse back. This continued despite the establishment of the Crewkerne Turnpike Trust in the 1760s, that trust adopting the main London Road from Stoke under Ham and widening it in the Chard direction on the other side of the town. The southern route was still considered to be easier on the horses, however, and an advertised extra enticement was that passengers could be shaved at Axminster by 'a lady barber.'

One should never leave Crewkerne without a visit to the museum. It stands in Market Square looking at the Town Hall and was founded as recently as 1988 in the former Council offices in Church Street, but was forced to close in 1994 when those premises became unsafe. Thanks to a lot of hard work, not to mention a grant from the Heritage Lottery, it was eventually rehoused in an old house in Market Square and opened by HRH The Princess Royal on 14 January 2000. The old Ham stone building makes an excellent background to what, inside, is an outstanding collection of memorabilia from the town's fascinating past.

FOUR

Crewkerne's Villages

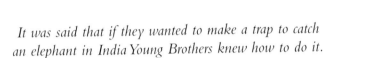

It was said that if they wanted to make a trap to catch
an elephant in India Young Brothers knew how to do it.

Pulman's Weekly News 1957

Crewkerne and Merriott may be close neighbours, but they are far from close friends on the football field. Matches between the rival teams once made Glasgow's Rangers-Celtic clashes look like Sunday school picnics in comparison. A suggestion back in the 1960s that the two clubs combine, becoming either Cruiett or Merkerne, never had a serious chance of getting off the ground.

Merriott's main street was once Crewkerne's link with the A303 but the re-routing of that connection along the A356 towards Norton sub Hamdon has taken most of the heavy traffic away from the village. What is left now has to face being 'calmed' although the car drivers are probably anything but that.

The attractive All Saints church, with a tower that is unusually short by Somerset standards, stands on a small knap. Parts of the tower date from the thirteenth century but much of the rest of the building is from the fifteenth or sixteenth centuries. A stone embedded in the vestry wall, said to portray fighting cocks, is thought to be from the twelfth century and possibly from an earlier building. Another attractive Ham Stone building is the Kings Head just below the church which dates from 1745 and may have got its name from a rush of Royal support when the news reached Merriott that Bonny Prince Charlie was on his way south.

Thought to be the oldest house in the village, the lovely, half-thatch, half-slate Highway Cottage between the church and the Kings Head is now a pottery where David Brown, besides the usual range of high fired

The Kings Head, Merriott, seen here in around 1906, is thought to have been built in 1745 (the year that Bonnie Prince Charlie landed in Scotland).

functional pottery and wheel-thrown as well as hand-built larger pieces, indulges in his own personal interest in teapots, examples of which make a visit well worthwhile.

Court Mill, one of once four mills in the village, is named as such at least as far back as 1573. It ceased grinding in the 1930s and its mill pond was filled in around 1960. The 'city centre' is The Knapp, a central cross road where a disastrous fire caused £1,000 of damage in 1897. It was started when old George England who ran a draper's business there, fell down the stairs one night. He dropped the oil lamp that he was carrying, starting the fire which destroyed the shop, his dwelling house, and three adjoining cottages. Inter-community rivalry was forgotten, because it was the Crewkerne Fire Brigade that hurried to the scene and stopped the conflagration from spreading to the many neighbouring thatched buildings. One curiosity at The Knapp was the moving of Batstone's shop which in its time had occupied three of the four corners of the cross roads. First it was at the bottom (south-east) corner, in 1921 in went north-easterly and later it crossed the main road in a north-westerly direction.

One of Merriott's more interesting characters was 'Old Blind Joe' who was said to deliver papers around the village without a dog in Edwardian days. Apparently he had no bother with giving the correct change despite his handicap.

A school attached to the church existed at least as early as 1618 when the vicar taught nine boys. References are made to teachers after that and the infants Board School was built in 1876 and the old Sunday school became a mixed Board School. The introduction of the comprehensive system meant that the pupils aged over nine were taught at Crewkerne after 1972. A new school was built later, the old school building being retained as a dining-room.

During the First World War Merriott's School, no doubt like many others, were more than active on the Home Front where its League of Young Patriots were busy collecting countryside commodities for hospitals and the military. By 1917 nearly 12,000 eggs had been sent to local hospitals, ninety-one walking sticks went to the wounded and the Royal Navy received as much as 25 cwt of apples and twenty-eight sacks bags of vegetables. There was also a School Savings Association which raised almost £1,400 in under two years.

To the north-west of Crewkerne, on the higher land that looks towards Merriott, one would have to go a long way to find a better, unspoilt village than Hinton St George. Its main street is a procession of beautiful old Ham stone buildings, either with thatch or slate, and, at the western end of the village, St George's parish church is a building to savour even by Somerset's high standards. Perpendicular in style and dating from around 1225, the west tower was added towards the end of

Court Mills, seen here around 1933, was once one of four mills in Merriott. The mill pond was filled in during the 1960s for safety reasons.

the fifteenth century and the rest of the building followed in the fifteenth and sixteenth centuries. Inside almost all the memorials are to members of the Poulett family. One member of that illustrious family, however, William the seventh Earl, did have a brass plate placed beneath the window just inside the south door in memory of Charles Irish 'a trusted and faithful servant' who died in 1915.

The most impressive memorial is that of Sir Anthony Poulett and his wife, just inside the entrance to the chancel. He died in 1600 and lies with his wife on top of the tomb; both are surrounded by their ten children who can be seen kneeling around the base of the tomb, five of them looking towards the chancel. There is another reclining knight in front of the Poulett pew, said to be Sir John Denebaud, although others say that it is his son-in-law, Sir William Poulett, who died in 1488. Away from the memorials, which can be overpowering at times, there are some splendid Perpendicular arches and an attractive thirteenth-century font. The wagon roof ceiling is also exceptionally good.

Outside the church one should pause for a moment to admire the Rectory which dates from 1841 when the original building was considered to be unsafe. It was old when the benefice joined with Merriott. The Poulett Arms, the Hare and Hounds until 1824, has a Fives Wall at the rear. Fives was very popular in Ham stone country, several walls remaining, including those at Stoke under Ham and Shepton Beauchamp. At Martock on a buttress on the north side of All Saints' church, you can still see the foot holes cut to help players climb and recover balls that were 'lost' on the roof. Built of Ham stone, the Poulett Arms has been modernised inside but this in no way detracts from what a true village pub should look like. Between the pub and the church there is a late medieval, stepped village, or preaching, cross. The figure on its front is supposed to be that of John the Baptist, but no authority exists for this.

There are far too many exceptional houses in Hinton St George to list them all individually. But in South Street, its nineteenth-century Teapot Lane name, is thoughtfully retained in two adjacent cottages called Teapot Cottage and Teapot Garage. Not so historically thoughtful is a third cottage which goes under the name of Winnie the Pooh Cottage. At the end of Teapot Lane, Gas Lane takes you back towards the village cross. This lane takes its name from the fact that the village gas works stood there. Further on is Hinton House, now in private hands as you are warned by a notice at the entrance.

A handsome governess cart outside Ilford House in East Street, Merriott, c. 1907.

Before leaving Hinton, go back to the entrance to the church drive where the house facing the church (Gainsfords) was once the home (1925-1933) of Henry Fowler, the eminent compiler of *Fowler's Modern English Usage* and, no doubt the neighbours gossiped about why he was burning the midnight oil. Fowler was a teacher at a Sedbergh School in Yorkshire from 1882-1899 and started compiling dictionaries after he had left there. After service with the BEF in France in the First World War he moved to Somerset and completed the *magnus opus* that he had started working on with his brother, Francis George, in 1911. Francis died of tuberculosis contracted in France when he was also serving with the BEF.

We make no comment on the claim that Pumky Night, held in October, which sees people carrying hollowed out mangold lights, stems from the days when local women went in search of their husbands who were late in coming home from Chiselborough Fair. They ought to have first looked in the Poulett Arms or the George & Crown which was destroyed by fire in 1959.

He might one day have become the Chancellor of All England and, until he fell foul of Henry VIII, the most powerful man in the realm, but the young Thomas Wolsey had to spend time in the stocks like all the sixteenth-century equivalents of Lopen's lager louts. Lopen is a small hamlet to the north of Merriott and it was there that Sir Amias Poulett, enraged at the youthful Wolsey's excesses of wine on a feast day, put him in the stocks where, no doubt like any other common malefactor, he was pelted with rubbish. Wolsey had the last laugh. When he became Chancellor he ordered Sir Amias not to leave the City of London without his permission. After a later act of contrition, he was forgiven but, being only human, he most have smiled at Wosley's subsequent downfall.

Lopen once had two inns, three if you count the Poulett Arms at Lopen Head, which you must, and also two schools. The first two inns, the King William Inn and the Crown, have closed, the Crown around 1950. The schools are known to have existed in 1819 but were teaching only thirty-seven children. A Sunday school flourished to such an extent in the nineteenth century, however, that at one time ten teachers were employed. William Forster's 1870 Education Act brought a state school to Lopen in 1879. At first there were over seventy pupils on the register but the numbers dwindled steadily throughout the twentieth century and in 1952 the school, down to thirteen junior pupils by the time it was closed.

Lopen is not the most attractive of the villages in Ham stone country, the busy road through its centre hardly helps. But there are some handsome Ham stone buildings to be found. Bridge Farm, a few yards away on the Merriott road is one. Others include Shores Farm in the village itself.

To the west of Lopen a straight and narrow lane, part of the Fosse Way after it has left the old line of the A303, takes you to Dinnington, a very small hamlet, with one of the few really old English pubs that has managed to escape the mindless 'modernising' whims of the brewers and also retained its olde worlde charm. The front door opens on to the Fosse Way but the Rose and Crown moves away from history when it claims, tongue in cheek we might add, that a few yards across the fields are the 'Dinnington Docks' where the Chard Canal ran. It would have been a wonderful feat of engineering if it climbed the land mass between it and that town. But a pub that sells real ale and doesn't mind if customers bring in the mud from outside on their feet can be forgiven most things.

This part of the Fosse Way serves as a rat run for East Devon taxi drivers plying the London airports run. The ordinary driver would either leave the A303 at the Norton junction, and head for home via Crewkerne and Windwhistle, or go on to Ilminster and then go home through Chard. The taxi men leave the trunk road at Lopen Head, dash along the lane through Dinnington and come out on the A30 where it begins its climb up to Windwhistle. Are they right? Throw the odd tractor or herd of cattle into the equation and they may not be.

Misterton is home to Crewkerne's station and it is also one of the very few places that has a 20 mph speed limit in the village centre where the busy A356 snakes its way around a series of narrow corners on its way to Dorchester. Away from that road St Leonard's church was completely rebuilt in 1840 in Church Lane. There are some attractive Ham stone buildings in that area, including Old Court, home of the Spoures family for over two centuries from 1399. Henry Parsons, who lived at Misterton Manor House towards the end of the nineteenth century, was a man of many parts, including being the agent for the Portman estates in Somerset and Dorset and Lord Wolvisiton's Dorset properties. He also served as a director to the *Western Chronicle* newspapers, the Wilts and Dorset bank and Crewkerne Breweries. In his younger days he played rugby for Somerset and went on to serve as a member of the Chard RDC and became a JP for eleven years, during which time he was chairman on the Crewkerne Bench. In more recent times Helen Mathers, the authoress of *Comin' thro' the Rye* and other novels was born in Misterton.

An unusual business that once flourished just off the A3066 beyond Misterton towards North Perrott was that of Young & Sons (Misterton) Ltd which was founded by Samuel Young in 1896. His fours sons, Frederick George, William Charles, Sidney and George following in father's footsteps in due course. They made vermin traps and exported them all over the world. It was said that if they wanted to make a trap to catch an elephant in India, Young Brothers knew how to do it. They also made fishing lines and nets which were exported as far as the Cook Islands and, among their more unusual orders was one from Ireland for nets to catch falcons, strictly illegal today of course. As only to be expected from a country firm, they made a considerable number of rabbit traps, a trade which received a severe setback when the myxomatosis epidemic played havoc with Britain's rabbits in the 1950s.

North Perrott is separated from the larger South Perrott by the Somerset-Dorset county boundary. Both take their name from the River Parrett which rises just a few yards inside Dorset to flow northwards and join the Yeo at Langport in the Somerset Levels.

North Perrott straddles the A3066 which enables traffic heading for Bridport to bypass Crewkerne. On that main road, Middle Street, the

Manor Arms once had a handsome sign board bearing the Hoskyns coat of arms and family motto *Finen respice* (Look towards the end). It was so frequently a victim of passing lorries that it was taken down in 1957 and placed on the village green opposite the inn.

St Martin's church, almost a twin of its South Perrott neighbour, lies off the main road to the west along the lane that leads to North Perrott Manor, now Perrott Hill School, a private establishment founded in 1946 and standing in a large ornamental park.

St Martin's is a cruciform, mainly Perpendicular, building which was largely rebuilt around the end of the fourteenth century. The lane to it is lined with tall beech trees which tended to make the approaches dark in winter, so dark in fact that the rector, Revd Dashwood, placed an oil lamp there in the 1920s. There was a studded lych gate to the churchyard with hand-forged hinges where another lamp was placed. Inside that it was a slightly uphill walk to the church which is surrounded by cyclamen, a beautiful sight in late autumn when they are in flower. They probably surpass the famous cyclamen at Alphington church near Exeter.

Somerset has many lovely, even quaint, place names. Midsomer Norton, Keinton Mandeville, Kingsbury Episcopi and Bower Hinton spring to mind among others. Another is Haslebury Plucknett, tucked away just off the A30 a mile or so after it leaves Crewkerne on the way

The White Horse, Haslebury Plucknett, c. 1910.

74

The Railway Hotel, Newton, Martock, c. 1946. The hotel was built in the 1860s to cater for the railway trade.

to North Perrott. The name comes from two entirely separate parts of the village's history. Haselbury is a corruption of the Halberd of the Domesday Book (1087) and its origins are said to be from the Saxon (O.E.) Haesel bearu or hazel grove. The Plucknett came later, and it is another corruption, this time of Plugenett, an Alan Plugenet being granted a charter for a weekly market in the village by Henry III (1216-1272).

Haslebury straggles too much to be as pretty as many of its neighbours, probably due to much post-war development, but there is still some handsome Ham stone to be found. Especially on the outside of the church of St Michael and All Angels, inside, however, it is a different matter. The first thing that most people note when they visit the church for the first time and approach it from the lane are the two clock faces on the fourteenth/fifteenth-century tower with its two battered looking effigies on either side of the west door. Unusually the clock face looking out from the west wall of the tower is some ten feet lower than the clock face that looks to the east. The clock was installed around 1879 and was fitted with new electric gear in 1974 in memory of Arthur Spore.

We know new things are bound to look new and the west gallery is at least functional and the new woodwork in and around the vestry greatly adds to both its security and looks. But those three stained glass windows on the south wall, said to represent the birth of Christ, the Transfiguration and the Resurrection and Penteos, look rather like the images seen through the kaleidoscopes that were very popular among children in the

1930s inside of which pieces of coloured glass were shaken around to give various images of colour. Artistic licence is all very well, especially in a day and age when a pile of bricks is said to be art. But the windows at St Michael's could just as easily be said to represent a sunset, a sunrise, or Krakatoa in eruption.

Long before those windows arrived, Wulfric, a priest from Compton Martin, arrived at Haslebury in 1125 to seek a life of solitude and to spend the rest of life in solitary prayer. Before he died some twenty-nine years later his modest and holy demeanour soon attracted pilgrims in search of his blessing. Legend has it that Henry I (1100-35) brought his queen, Matilda, with him to visit the recluse and that Stephen (1135-54) also brought his queen, another Matilda, to Haslebury. Despite all his piety and fame, however, Wulfric was never canonised although the celebrated itinerant John Leland mentions his tomb. His relics vanished during the Civil War when Cromwellian iconoclasts also destroyed much of the stained glass and church furnishings.

To the south of Crewkerne, where the B3165 crosses the River Axe a few yards away from Dorset, Clapton does not have a lot going for it. A disused mill, on the same site since 1228, a closed pub, the Blue Boy, and a few houses that have to put up with the noise and grime of traffic hurrying along its way to the Channel at Seaton or Lyme Regis. Most of them miss the only two things of interest about the place. Clapton Court, which is actually at Seaborough and in Dorset, and a small sign that says '13th Century Church.' Make sure you do not miss the sign nor the church which is at Wayford, about a mile up a narrow lane from where it looks out between the trees at the Axe valley below it. Wayford is not mentioned in Domesday, the first known reference to it being in 1206 in the *Curia Regis* Rolls. The tiny St Michael's church stands at the side of the Tudor Manor House with a small Priest's house looking over the Churchyard. Interestingly, the Manor House has been partly retiled in imitation Ham stone. It was rebuilt by Giles Daubeney in 1602 and E-shaped, as most Elizabethan houses were, to compliment (an euphemism for flattering) Queen Elizabeth I.

The first-known rector at St Michael's was John de Offele in 1339. In 1971, however, the living was joined with Crewkerne whose vicar now doubles as the rector of Wayford. A memorial on the south wall is to John Frederick Pinney (d.1762), the MP for Bridport whom, it calls, 'a man of flowing courtesy to all men.'

An outing to Bridport from Haslebury Plucknett, c. 1905. The house on the left is still much the same but the cottages on the right have had their thatch replaced with slates.

It is well worth risking meeting a tractor in the long and narrow lane that leads to Wayford and having to reverse. St Michael's is a lovely little place with, unusually, wooden pillars that were replaced during a 1902 restoration with pillars whose comparative newness is not apparent. The horse box pews are dark, and untidily attractive, although those in between the single aisle and the north wall are new. The darkness of the wood contrasts nicely with the whitewashed interior. Overhead the wooden roof is more in keeping with a barn than a church, but that does not in any way detract from the air of serenity inside a remarkable building. The Royal Arms over the north door are those of George III (1760-1820). Wayford is not even a small hamlet, just a huddle of houses straddling a lane with, on the last electoral roll, twenty-nine voters - and the polling booth would have still had to stay open all day.

That lane is part of the Jubilee Trail which runs along the Axe Valley from Crewkerne before looping south towards Lyme Regis. Also running out of Crewkerne the Monarch's Way ends at Charmouth where Charles II ended up after the Battle of Worcester (1651).

Having taken the trouble to drive up the lane, take a bit more and walk the few hundred yards to Wayford woods where the Baker family established the famous collection of rare rhododendrons and camellias. It is well worth it when the flowers are in bloom.

FIVE

The Cokers
and Chinnocks

I have sung in the Albert Hall, St Paul's Cathedral,
York Minster, Lincoln Cathedral, every cathedral
in the south-west and Midlands, in its own peaceful
and beautiful way this church matches them all.

Visitors' book at All Saints' church
at Sutton Bingham

The Chinnocks and the Cokers, buried down long and narrow lanes, are Somerset at its best. Especially West Chinnock where, with Chinnock Brook gurgling its way to the still infant, nearby Parrett, apart from a tractor chugging happily through the straggling village, the only thing to disturb the rural calm is the buzz of helicopters using the old wartime RAF station at Merrifield on the other side of the A303.

It would be hard to say where to start in a village crammed full of handsome buildings, one of the better of which is High Cross, dated 1604, although that might be the date of a rebuilding. It stands at the top of the village where the road branches for either Yeovil (Duckpool Lane) or deeper into the countryside at Chiselborough (East Lane). There is a well in the middle of the junction. For obvious reasons, much of the building in Ham stone country has weathered to a dull brown, even muddy brown where those by a main road have fallen foul of the passing traffic. But, if you want to see it as it was when the villages were in the mornings of their glory, go a few yards along Duckpool Lane and the brilliant, warm brown, Ham stone almost dazzles the eye in a brand new housing estate.

Coker Court workforce, complete with the estate's own fire brigade, c. 1905.

Running proud with St Mary's church is Church Close, which the casual passer-by, with some justification, might decide are alms houses with delightful lattice windows. In fact they were built by Richard Hayward in around 1840 for his weavers. Hayward is remembered inside St Mary's church by a stained glass window dated 1852. Victorian restoration in 1889-90 has left the interior much less attractive than it is outside where the unusual saddle back tower always commands a second look. Unusually the church has three separate gateways, two of them providing a handy short cut to villagers in the know.

Tiny and unspoilt Middle Chinnock lies just to the east of its larger neighbour and is full of Ham stone. Like most of its neighbours it was given to Robert, Count of Mortain after the Conquest.

East Chinnock, however, is anything but unspoilt, standing as it does on the A30, although it does have one thing in its favour; two farms both selling cider. Also in its favour is the parish church of the Blessed Virgin Mary, a popular dedication in this part of Somerset. The thing that catches most eyes on entry are the stained glass windows, all but one the work of a German prisoner of war, Gunther Anton, who was placed in the POW Camp at Houndstone near Yeovil after being shot down during a raid on the Southampton docks in 1944. By 1945 he was working on a farm at East Chinnock. On his return to Stuttgart in 1948 he joined his father in making and restoring stained glass windows. Wanting to repay the village where he had been made to feel at home and also the church where he often prayed, Gunter returned to England in 1962 with a new window for the south wall of the nave. Over the next twenty-six years he would provide stained glass for all the other windows of the church except the east window which retains its Victorian glass and is a memorial to a former churchwarden. His last gift was the unusual tower screen which is made of glass bricks with *Agnus Dei* and the Banner of Victory covering some of the bricks above the door. To the right is a small brass plaque with the names of Gunther and three other German POWs. Despite the stained glass, the interior of St Mary's is very light and cheerful.

Moving eastwards we come to the Cokers and Sutton Bingham on the outskirts of Yeovil. The furthest east is Sutton Bingham which no longer exists as such. Not that it ever amounted to very much. In 1840 its population was just seventy-eight and in 1955, when most of the tiny village was drowned to create the 142-acre reservoir that supplies the Yeovil area with its water and after seven cottages (actually they were first demolished) were drowned, only about five or six, along with the church and manor house remained. Twenty-five years later there were only ten addresses in the parish. Sutton Bingham reservoir's catchment area is almost 7,500 acres, the main supply being the two anonymous

A pleasant, almost idyllic, country scene that was about to be completely changed for all time. This was 1950 and about a year later work began on constructing the 142-acre Sutton Bingham Reservoir that would hold up to 575 million gallons when completed.

arms of a tributary of the Yeo which flow either side of Halstock to meet almost at the reservoir itself. Neither have a name but both rise in Dorset, the western arm on the slopes below Winyard's Gap, the eastern near Corscombe. Both contribute to Sutton Bingham's 575 million gallon capacity although, being a lowland reservoir, it is not particularly deep. Divers who have gone down into it reckon that it is literally impossible to see your hand in front of your face under the surface. The waters are kept back by a 43-ft high dam which stretches for 1,000 ft across the valley. During the 1975 drought there was only six weeks water supply left in the reservoir, and in 1990 the level was so low that it looked more like a small river than a 142-acre lake and some former inhabitants went back to see if they could find any traces of their old homes. Four of the families were rehoused in new council houses. John and Amelia House, who had lived at different times with their seven children in two of the houses, were the last to leave.

Today there is pleasant picnic area, fishing, mainly for rainbow or brown trout, from either the bank or a boat, and a bird-watching hide on the southern arm which overlooks the conservation area. Sutton Bingham is home to many varieties of water fowl, and is an important station for many migrant species including ospreys in the spring and autumn. Shaped like an axe with its blade facing east, the tip of the handle is in Dorset near Halstock, the county boundary still faithfully following its 'pre-drowning' path which can be seen on the Ordnance Survey map half crossing the southern tip and then making a dog-leg bend back on its self just before it reaches the other bank. The reservoir lies in a wooded basin with Birts Hill to the west – the highest point of the surrounding hills. Standing at 182 metres (597ft), much of the hill is covered by Pen Wood and bisected by the county boundary.

The Sutton Bingham story is thought to have been the inspiration for Cecil Day Lewis's (Poet Laureate 1969-72) poem 'Seen From the Train'. The case for the defence rests on the fact that there were cedar trees near the church in the poem as there are at Sutton Bingham. For the prosecution, however, the church in the poem was later flooded

But All Saints' church at Sutton Bingham was not. In fact conservationists would have been up in arms at the very mention of such a suggestion. It is a unique little church standing behind the picnic area on the west bank. To reach it you take the short lane off the Halstock road after crossing the bridge at the top end of the reservoir.

Perhaps the words of John Whatley, written in the Visitors' Book in 1986 best sums up the place. He was a member of St Mary's choir at Redcliffe, Bristol, and his words are, ' I have sung in the Albert Hall, St Paul's Cathedral, York Minster, Lincoln Cathedral, every cathedral in the south-west and Midlands, in its own peaceful and beautiful way this church matches them all. Please keep it alive and well.'

Once inside you will share John Whatley's feelings. A Norman church with its original beautiful Norman arch leading into the chancel, it is not just simply beautiful, but beautifully simple. Even the barn-like wooden ceiling adds to the beauty. When the roof of the nave was restored in around 1955 some of the original, elm timbers were in such good condition that they were re-used.

All Saints' is believed to have been built around 1111 and partly rebuilt about 1300. Despite it smallness there is so much to see there and, although it is always best to start at the beginning, in All Saints' case the north porch, the parts that attracts most attention are the wall paintings and the chancel arch The latter is three arches made into one, the inside one supported on jambs in the shape of semi-circular pillars. The other arches are supported on jambs of free-standing circular columns. It is thought that it once served as the entrance to another building which

The road that leads from the centre of Stoke under Ham up to Ham Hill and the stone quarries around 1906.

was taken into the church during the 1300 rebuilding. This contention is borne out by the fact that the arch is only visible when looking into the chancel from the nave, looking back once in the nave all one sees is the shape of an arch.

The church's original dedication was to St Mary, a dedication that was not too popular in Henry VIIIs time, and the change was made to All Saints'. It is St Mary, however, who is the subject of most of the medieval wall paintings on the walls of the church which most likely date from the 1300 rebuilding. The best painting is on the centre of the north wall of the nave and contains two pictures. On the left the death of the Virgin Mary is depicted, on the right she is seen being carried away on a bier. In the first picture the Apostles and Jesus surround her bed; St John stands at her feet holding a palm leaf, said to have been given to her by an angel as a warning of her imminent death. This painting was uncovered around the time of the First World War, those in the chancel around 1868, including the most important one, the 'Crowning of the Virgin by our Lord.'

The church guide on sale inside All Saints' laments the fact that 'the paintings have been referred to as crude.' And rightly so. Would anyone use such an adjective when describing the cave paintings at Lascaux in France?

The north porch also has a Norman arch although the door, which may have been later replaced, is thirteenth century in style. There was once a south door but it was half filled in and changed into a window. The Norman presence can also be found in the western end of the nave where there are two windows in the traditional shape of that period. In the eastern end the windows were rebuilt around 1300. The Norman font in the nave is a very good example of its period although, unusual for the time, it is circular.

There are two bells, the larger one dated 1685, being cracked and no longer in use. The smaller of the two, however, has to be one of the oldest church bells in Somerset dating as it does from around 1250. Both bells are housed in thirteenth-century arches.

In the early 1990s Sutton Bingham's living was joined with East Coker and Closworth which means that the priest in charge is a rector when he is at Sutton Bingham but a vicar when he goes back to St Michael's at East Coker which is two miles over the hill to the west of Sutton Bingham. It was the birthplace (at Hymerford House) of the celebrated navigator and writer Captain William Dampier in 1651. Dampier, whose memorial plaque can be seen in St Michael's parish church, was a colourful character. If he had been asked to fill out his CV he could have written, under previous experience, explorer, geographer, navigator, naval captain and writer. Dampier circumnavigated the globe three times and was the first Englishman to set eyes on Australia and explore it. He landed on the north-west coast of that continent in 1688 and again in 1699 when, in command of one of HM ships under orders to explore New Holland as the country was then called. And all this some seventy years before Captain Cook set foot there. Dampier was a mariner of the old school, his experiences at sea including voyages to Newfoundland, Bantam, Jamaica and Campeachy Bay. He spent two years among the lawless wood-cutters of Yucatan (Mexico) and, in 1679, he crossed Darien with them. In 1683 he sailed from Sierra Leone for Chile and then on across the Pacific where he was marooned on Nicobar Island. From there he eventually made his way in a native canoe to Acheen and returned to England in 1691 to write his celebrated *Voyage Around the World*. He had not lost the wander bug and soon he was off to the South Seas again where his name is with us today in the Dampier Archipelago and the Dampier Strait. Shipwrecked at Ascension Island on his way home, both he and his crew survived for two months on turtles and goats.

The workforce at Drake's webbing factory, c. 1910. The factory has long since closed and a housing estate stands on its site. Happily the name Drake is retained in that estate. It is said that another factory in the village manufactured the sailcloth for Nelson's flagship the Victory.

The brass plate which commemorates this famous son of East Coker, on the wall of the parish church, bears the following inscription:

Buccaneer, Explorer, Hydrographer and sometime Captain of the ship Roebuck in the Royal Navy of King William III. Thrice he circumnavigated the Globe and, first of all Englishmen, explored and described the coast of Australia. An exact observer of things in Earth, Sea and Air, he recorded the knowledge won by years of danger and hardship in Books of Voyages and a Discourse on Winds, Tides and Currents, which Nelson bade his midshipmen to study and Humbolt praised for scientific worth. Born at East Coker 1651, he died in London 1715, and lies buried in an unknown grave. The World is apt to judge of everything by the success, and who so ever has ill fortune will hardly be allowed a good name.

The then High Commissioner of Australia, Mr T.W. White, was among those present at a service to mark the tercentenary of Dampier's birth in September 1951 and said of him, 'We can all agree that he measured up with Drake and Raleigh, Cook and Flinders, and has brought added lustre to this imperishable Britain.'

William Dampier is not the only great man whose memorial can be found in St Michael's. Thomas Stearns (T.S.) Eliot (1888-1965), the famous American playwright, poet and literary critic, who was born in St Louis, Missouri, on 26 September 1888, is also there. He came to Britain to study at Merton College, Oxford, before the First World War and, staying on after that war, fell so deeply in love with the country from which his forebears had emigrated that he became a British subject and, in 1948, became a member of the Order of Merit and also won the Nobel Prize for Literature.

Among his best known works are *Murder in the Cathedral*, *The Family Reunion* and *The Cocktail Party*. His children's poems, *Old Possum's Book of Practical Cats* formed the basis for Andrew Lloyd Webber's musical *Cats* in 1981. He wrote many poems, one of the most famous being called 'East Coker', the opening and closing lines of which, 'In my beginning is my end... in my end is my beginning', are engraved upon his memorial.

The admirable booklet, *T.S. Eliot, Poet, 1888-1965*, which is on sale inside St Michael's church, tells us that there were about eighty signatures in the Visitors Book in 1964, the year before Eliot's ashes were buried there. In 1982 over 700 people recorded their thoughts, many of them drawn there because of his presence and their love of his works.

Eliot's ancestors sprang from East Coker, there being a reference to the family name there as early as 1563. Later an Andrew Eliot emigrated to America from the village in around 1660. Possibly he left Somerset because of his religious beliefs, the seventeenth century was a time of much upheaval in English religion. If so it is perhaps ironic that he was to settle in Salem where he was on the jury for the famous, some might prefer infamous, Salem Witch Trials.

But there is more to see at St Michael's than just the memorials to William Dampier and T.S. Eliot. It is a superb church, in superb surroundings, and, although the earliest documentary references to it are late thirteenth century, there was almost certainly a church here in Saxon times and, if the Norman font inside can be used in evidence, the Normans quickly replaced that with one of their more solid stone buildings from the local Ham stone. Inside there is some good woodwork including the medieval wagon roof, three extra panels being put in the east end of the nave after the removal of the central tower at the end of the eighteenth century.

The brass lectern marks Queen Victoria's Diamond Jubilee (1897), the money needed being raised by subscription, and the Royal coat of arms above the north door which bear the date 1690 are those of William and Mary with the initials W and M intertwined. The original Charles II coat of arms were found underneath during recent restoration work.

When the central tower was removed because of its dangerous condition, a new tower was built at the east end of the church where the Chantry chapel of the Holy Cross had stood. There are eight bells inside that tower, all cast by Bilbies from Cullompton. The bells were cast before the old tower was removed which suggested the church authorities were planning ahead. During the life of the old tower there were only five bells at St Michael's and the bell ringers standing between the congregation and the altar was, to say the least, a great distraction. It would have been an even greater distraction in 1760 at the time of George III's Coronation when, it is said, the ringers drank forty gallons of cider. But perhaps the congregation helped out – forty gallons for five ringers would be sixty-four pints each! And cider would have been real cider in those days.

Especially impressive is the war memorial in Ham stone.

Garden Row, East Coker, c. 1902. The post office in the left background is still in use. Immediately in front of it but out of sight, Chapel Row, built in 1784, is said to the first purpose-built workhouse in the country.

There is a strong connection between East Coker and the Courtenay Earls of Devon who once held the advowson. They also owned Coker Court for over 300 years, and there are traces of the family's coat of arms inside St Michael's in the south transept window. There are also traces of the arms of the Diocese of Exeter who, upon granting permission for the erection of a chantry chapel in Exeter Cathedral where Mass could be said daily for the souls of Hugh Courtenay, second Earl of Devon, and Margaret his wife and other members of the family, accepted the transfer of the advowson of East Coker. From that date St Michael's had a vicar and not a rector, the first known rector having been Robert de St Nicholas in 1297.

St Michael's stands above the tiny village in an area many of the village's better buildings can be found. These include Paddock Cottage opposite the church, although it is rather grand for as cottage, Townsend Farm, Tellis Farm, Bubspool House and the Helyar Arms, a fine old country inn said to date from around 1460.

The Helyar family connection with East Coker began in 1616 when William Helyar, Archdeacon of Barnstaple and Elizabeth Is Chaplin bought Coker Court and founded the Helyar Alms House on the path to both Coker Court and the church in 1640. The houses were originally for eleven women and one man but, today, the twelve dwellings have been reduced to nine.

A mile away from East Coker, North Coker is marked as separate on the Ordnance Survey map but the locals will tell you that it is two separate places that have become one. Someone forgot to tell everybody because the post office calls itself East Coker and the nearby school goes by the name of North Coker.

There was once a St Luke's chapel at 'North' Coker, a chapel-of-ease to St Michael's. It was closed around 1992 and is now a private house. The Gospel Hall, at the end of Burton Lane, is a plain, well maintained mainly wooden building. St Francis of Assisi would have liked the place, almost every ridge tile on the roof seems to be a home to a pair of sparrows in the breeding season. Opposite the lane that leads to St Luke's, Burton Cottage Farm is a lovely Ham stone cottage with a whitewash plastered front. It has two buttresses facing the road and two lovely mullioned windows. The thatched roof has a hog back curve at one end.

East Coker (or North Coker) is hidden away in leafy and delightful Somerset countryside at its best. Much of West Coker stands in full view of the public on the main A30 some two miles to the west of Yeovil, although the parish church, dedicated to St Martin of Tours, a fourth century saint stands in a quiet part of the village.

Somerset justly has a reputation for having more than its fair share of lovely, and tall, church towers. St Martin's is one exception to the rule. The church itself is not all that high, the west tower, if not squat, is surely one of the lowest in the county. Originally the tower may have been even lower, the church guide on sale inside tells that 'until 1765 the tower was low and thatched'. There is a ring of eight bells, five thought to date from 1770 when they were either cast or recast by Thomas Bilbie, a member of the Cullompton family who cast the bells at East Coker. The other three bells were added later.

There are few windows in the church which leads to the dark, some might say gloomy, interior where the lights are usually left burning throughout the day. There has been a church here since at least Norman times, the tower could well date from then, parts of the nave are very early thirteenth century, and the chapel dates from 1360. The south aisle is as recent as 1830.

The rather fine reredos were given by the Revd William Laurence Cotter, a former rector, and his wife, in 1930. In this year in which Elizabeth II celebrated her Golden Jubilee, it might be of more than passing interest that the carpet of the High Altar is not only golden, but it once formed part of the carpet used in Westminster Abbey in 1953 for Her Majesty's Coronation.

Nearby Odcombe's most famous son was probably Tom Coryate who introduced the fulcifer (table fork) to England from Italy during the reign of James I (1603-25) and demonstrated how it would take the place of fingers. It also brought about a revolution in English cookery because, previously, the English had used a spoon which necessitated most foods being mashed and mixed together. He was ridiculed at first but the habit caught on because it was now possible to eat simple dishes and to eat both food dry and, most important of all, eat hard food, thus providing roughage and strengthening the teeth, a factor which, along with the improved dietary habits, Mead claimed in *The English Mediaeval Feast*, led to a considerable improvement in the life expectations during the Tudor Period.

South of the Cokers, where the county border marches proud with Dorset, the countryside opens out and although far from treeless, it is more open, especially around Hardington Mandeville where the Church of St Mary stands above the road at the northern end of the village affording a superb view of the countryside towards the valley of the upper Parrett and beyond it to the hills around Crewkerne.

The original St Mary's dates from AD 878 when the advowson was held by Alfred the Great who can be seen in the stained glass window in the south wall next to the door. It was a gift of Gilbert Rendell in memory of his parents Edward (1849-1926) and Elizabeth (1855-1929). The window was dedicated in 1990 by the Lord Bishop of Bath and Wells, the Rt Revd Dr George Carey. At the same time a window behind the font was given by the Rendell family in memory of George, another son of Edward and Elizabeth Rendell.

SIX

Stoke, Norton, Marton and South Petherton

When Ham Stone hears the Norton chimes at midnight clack
It rolls down the hill to drink at Jack o' Beards and back

Local saying

Stoke sub Hamdon is a village that has gone upmarket in as far as its name is concerned. It was Stoke under Ham until around the 1940s. One hesitates to claim that it was jealous of its smaller neighbour Norton who has the sub Hamdon tacked on to its name. But, whatever the reason for the change, Stoke under Ham became Stoke sub Hamdon. It was Stoke Beauchamp after the Conquest when it passed from Robert Fitzlvo's hands to the Beauchamp family at Hatch (now Hatch Beauchamp).

The famous stone has been quarried from the 430ft Ham Hill that looks out above the village towards the Somerset Levels since Roman times. The Romans and all subsequent quarrymen turning the top of the hill into a tormented landscape that almost hides the remains of an ancient earthwork. Known as the Frying Pan, this earthwork was the site of a stonemasons' picnic on Shrove Tuesday. In the charabanc era Ham Hill and its panoramic views was a must for outings. The quarries were closed in the 1950s but reopened by Ray Harvey in 1982 and are now owned and worked by Montacute Estates Ltd.

Stoke became an important part of the Yeovil glove-making industry during the eighteenth century. At one time there were as many as fourteen glove factories in the village, the earliest John H. Walter Ltd.

Stoke under Ham is actually two separate villages, West Stoke and the smaller East Stoke which is on the road to Montacute and where the Norman parish church of St Mary the Virgin can be found. The earliest parts of the building are the chancel and the nave are from around 1100

The road that leads from the centre of Stoke under Ham up to Ham Hill and the stone quarries around 1906.

George VI receiving Duchy of Cornwall tenants at Stoke under Ham shortly after becoming King in 1936.

The Bent Tree Café, Haslebury Plucknett, c. 1936.

George VI visiting the Ham Hill stone quarries in 1937, which were Duchy of Cornwall property at the time.

and form the earlier church which was without transepts or a tower. The font and lower tower date from later in the twelfth century. The chancel arch, remarkably like the one at Sutton Bingham, is Norman but said to have been rebuilt and also rebuilt again in 1857. The first known vicar was Osbert (1218).

Stoke under Ham produced a remarkable football team in the 1930s that won the championship of the Perry Street League five times in a row from the 1933–34 season. During those five seasons they won ninety-two of the 109 league games that they played; thirteen were drawn and only four lost. They scored 490 goals, conceding just 107 – an average of 5–1 a game.

William the Conqueror gave the manor of Stoke under Ham and Norton sub Hamdon to his half-brother, Robert, Count of Mortain, who passed Norton on to the monks at Grestern in Normandy. Henry V handed it to the de la Pole family when he alienated the foreign monasteries.

All that remains of the manor house at Norton sub Hamdon after it was demolished in the middle of the nineteenth century is the dovecote which now stands just inside the church gate. Pigeons were a valuable part of the medieval diet, being a source of fresh flesh for the larder in the long winter months when the palates of the upper classes were

Little Norton Mill, Norton sub Hamdon, c. 1905.

becoming jaded with salt. The house contained 400 nests, comes complete with its own pair of dormer windows and once had a wooden staircase for servicing the nests.

St Mary The Virgin's, certainly one of Somerset's better churches, dates from the fifteenth century, although there are traces of the earlier Norman building to be seen. Unusually tall, standing as it does at 98ft, 6ins, the magnificent tower was gutted by fire when it was struck by lightning on 29 July 1894. At the same time, the five bells in the tower were destroyed. Four of the bells dated from 1608 and were the work of the well known bell founder Richard Purdue of Closworth. The fifth bell was even older dating from the reign of Henry VIII (1509-1547). The restoration work took only twelve months to complete and included a ring of six new bells cast by the London firm of John Warner & Co. One of the memorials inside is to George Tanner, a twenty-seven-year-old private in the 19th Hussars, who died of fever on 19 February 1900 during the Siege of Ladysmith. It was built by subscription of 'his fellow villagers.'

A old saying in Norton claims:

When Ham Stone hears the Norton chimes at midnight clack
It rolls down the hill to drink at Jack o' Beards and back.

Water Street, Norton sub Hamdon, c. 1929. For some reason this lovely part of the village had its name changed to Little Street despite the fact that a clear, fast-flowing stream runs down its left-hand side.

The old post office at Norton sub Hamdon in 1904. Standing on the corner of Great Street and Water (now Little) Street, the building stills exist but has been divided into two separate houses and lost its thatch.

One hopes that not all the Ham stone sitting above the village hears the chimes, otherwise the village would be buried under several hundred tons of the stuff! Jack o' Beards is the name of a field halfway between the summit of Ham Hill and Norton, its considerable slope makes it a popular venue for youthful sledgers when there is snow around.

Chiselborough lies between Norton and West Chinnock and is referred to in Domesday as Ceoselbergon or gravel hill, a clear reference to its position in the shadow of Ham Hill from where the material came to make most of the dwellings in an attractive little place. After William the Conqueror won England at Hastings in 1066 he also gave Chiselborough to his Count of Mortain half-brother. It passed through several hands until John Wadham possessed it. It was shared out by his family in the seventeenth century.

Martock is said to be one of the biggest parishes in Somerset. It stands where the southern edge of the Levels meet the higher ground towards Yeovil Its name is said to be a corruption of Merstoc (OE) meaning a place near water, a probable reference to its proximity to those Somerset Levels which were much wetter at the time.

The town once sent its products the length and breadth of the United Kingdom, H.W. Hebditch & Co. Ltd being probably the country's leading manufacturer of wooden buildings and specialising in poultry and general farm buildings. The company had been formed in 1900 by

95

All Saints' church at Martock, c. 1920. Note the gas standard.

the Hebditch brothers, Harry and Charles, who began their working lives at South Petherton where they collected eggs from the farms. To cut out the expense of the middlemen as much as possible, and to ensure a regular supply of eggs, they also kept their own birds for which they made their own chicken houses. Local farmers noticed the quality of the houses to such an extent that the brothers set up in business with three generations of the family manuafacturing wooden buildings at Martock until the business ceased trading in 1985. It almost goes without saying that Hebditch's first offices were made of wood.

Martock's famous cricketing vicar, Revd A.P. Wickham, Archie or Wickers to all lovers of Somerset Cricket Club at the end of nineteenth century, was an outstanding wicket-keeper, perhaps the best the county ever had. His most memorable match was at Bristol when the legendary W.G. Grace scored his 100th first-class century. In all he made 288 and so little got past his bat that Wickers claimed in exasperation, 'I might just as well have stayed at home in Martock and prepared my sermon.'

He was a natural number eleven batsman, with a career best score of twenty-eight, and remembered for his curious stance when keeping wicket. He kept his legs apart and seldom stood at right angles to the bowler, a habit which modern coaches would have knocked out of him and thus condemning him to remain a nobody. Few of England's churches have stained glass windows with cricket stumps depicted on them. They do at East Brent, where Archie took the living for many years and where the congregation put up a window to commemorate a popular parson.

One of his more unusual claims to fame is that he is the only man to have kept wicket for both sides in a first class match. In 1901, when Somerset were playing at Oxford, the University keeper was injured while batting. They had no replacement and Wickham stood for them as well.

Archie would have loved the Church of All Saints at Martock, everyone who visits it does. Mainly fifteenth century, although there are traces of an earlier, thirteenth-century cruciform building. It was narrower than its successor and lost its central tower during the rebuilding. The new church owes its imposing looks and size to the flourishing cloth trade and the money that it brought.

One of the first things that strikes the first-time visitor is the finely carved roof which is dated 1513 on the strength of a shield bearing that date which was taken away and now hangs in the north chapel. The carvings on the tie-beams include petal flowers, crestings and angels with

The workforce at Sparrow's Engineering Works at Martock, pictured outside the factory entrance, c. 1915.

outspread wings. The roof above the nave was restored in the 1970s at a cost of nearly £70,000. All Saints suffered at the hands of Cromwell's iconoclasts who, in 1645, during the celebrations for the capture of nearby Bridgwater, smashed much of the glass and a fine organ.

The churchyard has two gates. Outside the south-west gate the stocks were placed after being repaired in 1936. On both the front and rear of the arch can be seen 'Robert Jeanes, Thomas Rowe, churchwardens, Anno Dn. 1627'. There is also a set of sundials. The names on the east gate have been damaged but those that can be identified include Thomas, R. W. Wardengs, Thomas Drent and Pittard and the date 1625. Both gates have been recently restored.

Unusually so, there are as many as seven scratch dials on the south wall, the purpose of which was to indicate the times of services. Happily clocks arrived before British Summer Time. The scratch dial on the west side of the porch seems to have been moved and placed (or replaced) in an upside-down position.

Opposite the church is one of the oldest inhabited houses in Somerset. Now known as the Treasurer's House, it is owned by the National Trust but not on regular view. Formerly it was the Manor House with a great hall dating from the very early thirteenth century. The cross wing may be even older.

Martock grammar school, founded 1661 and seen here around 1905.

Martock House in the 1920s when it was the meeting place of the ex-servicemen's Comrades Club. It has also been used as a fire station and for council meetings.

A few yards from the church on the corner of Pound Lane is the former grammar school which was converted from a court house in 1661 by William Strode of Barrington Court who was lord of the manor of Martock at the time. He demanded that the pupils only converse in Latin, both in school and outside. The school was closed in 1862 and became a private house during the 1970s.

The tall Martock House (*c.* 1770) is supported on pillars and blends nicely with the market cross or Pinnacle and the attractive houses that surround it. The Pinnacle was completely demolished by a lorry and had to be replaced. The Market House has had a varied life having been used as a fire station, a meeting place for the local council and other bodies, including the Comrades Club (a body of ex-servicemen).

The last train out of Martock station left for Taunton on 13 June 1964, the station, opened in 1862, being closed along with the rest of the Taunton-Yeovil former GWR line. Another form of transport first put in an appearance in the town in 1911 when the famous aviator Graham Gilmour flew a Bristol Boxkite version of the Farman pusher biplane from Larkhill, on Salisbury Plain, to Martock and gave flying demonstrations. A year later he was killed while flying back to London from Martock where he had been giving another display. Arthur Palmer. the son of a Martock farmer, had been offered a chance of flying with Gilmour but his father forbade him to go. No doubt Arthur took more notice of his father in future.

Many a 1950s and 60s courting couples around Ilminster will have happy memories of the H&C (Hutchings and Cornelius) coach company, often the only means of transport to dances and socials at

Baker & Sons were road contractors around the time of this picture (c. 1900) and are seen here at work in South Street, South Petherton.

neighbouring villages in the days before we all had cars. The firm began in 1930 when Alfred Cornelius, a stone mason who worked on the breakwaters at Portland, began operating a coach business from the Royal Oak at Barrington. In time he joined forces with Tommy Hutchings of South Petherton, the pair forming the company that was often (and irreverently) called 'Hot & Cold' or 'Horse & Cart.' The reason for the merger of the two businesses, both with five coaches, was the increase in purchasing power that it brought. The business closed in 1978.

Little Petherton in West Street was once almost a separate community where most of the inhabitants were far from wealthy; so far in fact that when the annual refuge collection took place some of the families sneaked out at night and took some of the wealthier peoples' rubbish and put it outside there own gates, thus giving the impression they were not that poor that they could not afford to throw anything away.

The thing that catches most people's eyes when they enter South Petherton's parish church of SS Peter & Paul is the Ayshe tomb in the vestry. There William Ayshe, Charles Is first Master of Horse during the Civil War, kneels with his mother Elizabeth, sister Hannah and two small boys. Cruciform in shape, SS Peter & Paul's was built around 1250 and rebuilt over 100 years later, though some of the older chancel was kept.

SEVEN

Ilminster and its Villages

⊶⊷

*As any back-door cider maker will tell you, the odd rat
or mouse in the cheese is what gives the cider 'its bite'*

Without any doubt, Ilminster's crowning glory is its minster dedicated
to St Mary, a popular dedication in this part of Somerset. St Mary's is not
only a magnificent building, it is matched by the beauty of its setting,
lovely old Ham stone buildings on all sides, but at a respectful distance.
Among the buildings there were once four houses built to accommodate
the four chantry priests. The priests, and their altars, vanished in the wake
of the Reformation, but two of the houses remain today. One is on the
west side, the other was converted into a grammar school in 1549.

In 1655 a writing master was appointed by the trustees who made
what appeared to be grants for elementary education. The school moved
to its present home in 1874 but fell foul of the Comprehensive
movement in 1971. Later it ceased to be a comprehensive school and
now, as the Greenfylde primary school, caters for the 5-9 years age
group. The earliest reference to a school in the town is of a boarding
school in 1440. Later, around 1670, a dame school was started at Horton.

Ilminster has its ghost; a girl at the grammar school who died of
diphtheria before her parents were able to arrive at her bedside. Claims
of sightings have been made. The town also had a witch called Mary
Hunt, a shadowy person who was buried at a cross road on the road from
Moolham past Oxenford Farm towards the main A358 road near
Hornsbury Hill. Another Ilminster tradition is that of its holy thorn, a
cutting from the original at Glastonbury, but we were unable to locate it.

The church building dates from the fifteenth century and one of the
better known of the thousands of worshippers to have entered the

church was James, ill-fated Duke of Monmouth in 1680, five years before he again briefly visited the town on his way to Sedgemoor and the axe on Tower Hill.

Lack of space for a growing congregation in the early years of the nineteenth century led to the introduction of large galleries on the north and south sides and also the west end. To make room for them the height of both the nave and the aisles were raised in 1824 and the pillars were raised on pedestals.

Of particular interest inside are the tombs in the Wadham Chapel in the north transept. One is of Sir William Wadham, who died in 1542, and his mother, Lady Joan Wadham. The other is of Nicholas and Dorothy Wadham. He was the founder of Wadham Collage at Oxford and was almost certainly born at Edge Barton at Branscombe between Seaton and Sidmouth in Devon. His mother Joan was a Tregarthin from Cornwall, a family whose six quarterings include that of King John's son Richard, the Plantagenet Earl of Cornwall. Joan was married twice, first to John Kellaway, who she bore fourteen children, and then John Wadham, and another six children including Nicholas.

Another tomb, this time in the south transept, in the Lady chapel, is that of Humphrey Walrond, a church warden, and a founder of Ilminster grammar school, who died in 1580. The brasses on both tombs are very striking, that on Nicholas's tomb is said to be the finest post-

Yandle & Son, Ilminster, c. 1905.

Messrs J. & E. Crouch's Station Road Garage, Ilminster, c. 1931. Still a garage but very much modernized and trading today as J. Brake & Son.

Reformation brass in England. The early perpendicular traceries around it are also well worth the trouble of a visit.

Entering the church through the West door, one has to then go through cut-glass doors placed there to mark the Millennium. Handsome enough, but some might think them out of place among all the lovely Ham stone on offer.

The tower is ninety feet tall with a peal of eight bells, the tenor bell, dating from 1732 and weighing in at 23 cwt, is one of the heaviest in the county. The oldest of the bells dates from 1583 but was recast in 1902. Two of the others date from the reign of James I (1603-25). Also dating from the reign of James I is the pulpit which was once three-tiered and stood on the south side of the church.

After meeting for some ten years in the Red Cross room at the rear of the George Hotel, the Catholic community built a new church, seating 110 people, in Station Road in 1954 at a cost of £3,250, half of the sum being raised by local worshippers.

The Duke of Monmouth may have been one of the most famous people to visit St Mary's, without doubt one of Ilminster's later visitors would become one of the most famous persons in the world. Brought there by her impoverished father, Edward Duke of Kent, who was fleeing to the West Country to escape his creditors, the infant Princess

Market Square, Ilminster, c. 1902. On the left, immediately past the entrance to Ditton Street, J. & E. Perry's, a furnishings and ironmongery store, is now a Red Cross charity shop.

Victoria spent Christmas Eve 1819 in the George Hotel in the town. Edward was on way to the seclusion of Woolbrook Cottage in Sidmouth and had stayed for a few days with his old, tutor, the Bishop of Salisbury to make arrangements to have his mail sent to him in an attempt to throw his creditors off the scent. The Kent family left for Sidmouth on Christmas Day but were not there for long, the Duke catching a cold which turned critical and he died on 23 January 1820, Victoria and her mother leaving for London where on arrival they learnt that the Duke's father, George III, had also died and his eldest son was now King as George IV and that Victoria was now heir to the throne.

For many years after the Wharf Lane Concrete Company (now Minster Stone) has crushed Ham stone to manufacture concrete products ranging from gate posts and fire places, to tomb stones and other memorials. Many British churches contain examples of its work. They had an international reputation, especially in the newly independent countries in Africa, where their exports included two fine cast concrete plaques bearing the arms of Sierra Leone which were sent from Tilbury Docks to Africa in 1962. On their arrival they were painted in the correct heraldic colours and the blocks, each four foot six inches in diameter and weighing three-quarters of ton, were fixed to the front of Government Building. The order had been placed with the Ilminster company by the Crown Agents for Overseas Governments and Administrations.

The height at which the plaques were to be fixed provided the carving staff with a challenging task to produce something which could be clearly seen at a distance. All they had to work on was a small design drawing and to make sure that the best results were achieved, the carvers set out the Coat of Arms to its full size and then made a plastic model which showed a good, deep relief. The work took six weeks in all.

The company owes it name to the fact that it began life in Wharf Lane, the road that led to the canal docks. It moved to a site in Station Road on the outskirts of the town and, when that area became a roundabout in a traffic improvement scheme in the 1990s it moved again, this time to a new industrial estate close by. Appropriately there is a new housing estate next door, sadly constructed in reconstituted Ham stone rather than the real thing.

A shovel can be seen hanging in Ilminster Square in pictures from around 1880. It was placed there to remove horse droppings.

The A303 on its way from the Ilminster bypass to climb the Blackdown Hills towards the Eagle Tavern and affords some superb views out over Vale of Taunton on the way, but no longer passes through Horton. A new bypass has seen to that and it makes life safer and quieter for the inhabitants.

An Ilminster school trip making its way down East Street in around 1905.

It is a small place, attractive enough away from the main road, no church, but a pub (the Five Dials), and no visible boundary with its bigger neighbour Broadway, one of south-west Somerset's better villages. The two neighbours are joined together by the local cricket club which bears the name of the Broadway & Horton CC.

There are so many buildings in Broadway worth a second look that it is hard to know where to start. We do so with the parish church of St Aldhelm and St Eadburgha, a very early dedication which suggests that a church existed here even before the reign of King Alfred (871–99). The church stands surrounded by fields almost a mile to the east of the village, the reason being, it is claimed, is that sixteenth-century plagues so reduced the numbers of inhabitants living around the church that, when the plague went away, no one wanted to live there and the village's centre moved to where it is today.

It is a small building, although there are two transepts, constructed mainly in either local Moolham stone or chert and flint with Ham stone used in the buttresses and quoins. The lichen covering both the church and most of its immediate tombs, and a preaching cross outside the south door (which has lost its arms), gives an attractive and ancient look to the place. Much of the interior, including the chancel and

Mr E. Crouch, driver for Yandle's Garage of New Street, Ilminster, collects a passenger from one of Ilminster's surrounding villages, c. 1908.

transepts, are from the thirteenth century but the nave and tower were rebuilt in the fifteenth. That interior is, possibly, somewhat austere but, thanks to the plain glass of the windows, remarkably light and cheerful. On either side of the doorway leading to the belfry there are wooden boards bearing the Ten Commandments, the Creed and the Lord's Prayer.

Broadway is a village on the way up again. In the 1841 census there were 618 inhabitants, by 1921 only 300 souls remained, but today there are almost 700 people living in the village. In the other direction, however, Broadway has lost its Congregation chapel, built in 1739 and closed in 1960, its bakehouses and its blacksmiths' forges, one of which stood opposite Yatford Cottage and is now the village stores. Much of the increase in population is housed in the newer buildings dotted around which have been sensibly blended in with their older neighbours. These neighbours include the almshouses, seven tenements provided for the poor of the parish provided in the will of Alexander Every who died in 1598. and left £100 for that purpose. The almshouses, however, were not constructed for another 100 years. Built of Ham stone and with a tiled roof, the seven dwellings, previously with one bedroom each, were reduced to three two-bedroomed and one single bedroomed dwelling in 1958.

Broadway Sunday school, 1911.

Broadway, c. 1900.

In the centre of the village there are some splendid old buildings including Stepp Farm with its leaded light windows, although its overgrown garden tends to spoil its appearance. Yatford Cottage and immediate neighbour, Shattrick House are probably the best of a very good bunch. Both are built in brick, the former with a tiled roof, Shattrick House with thatch.

Ashill, now bypassed by the re-routed A358 trunk road from the M5 which takes the traffic to south-west Somerset and East Devon, stands in flatter countryside, a conspicuous feature of which is the considerable amount of mistletoe to be seen on many of the trees. The parish church of St Mary's stands on a small knoll to the west of the village which it could look out over if it was not for the brick-built rectory opposite the school has that stands in the way. Two of the rectory's lancet windows have been bricked in, probably to avoid paying the Window Tax which was not abolished until 1851.

The church itself has Norman north and south doors, the north with its octagonal shafts being particularly interesting. Among the better things inside are the thirteenth-century window on the north side of the nave and the effigy of a woman wearing a wimple in a tomb recess close by. Above her is trefoiled gabled arch and there are two small

An unknown occasion in Broadway, c. 1905. Even as boys all the males are wearing the obligatory cap.

figures by her head. A smaller recess dates from the late 14th century and contains an effigy of a knight. Catching the eye are the large number of brightly coloured hassocks, some depicting special events such as the wedding of the Prince of Wales to Lady Diana Spencer, other, with their dedications and dedicators on the reverse, are either in floral and similar design and sometimes with a symbol associated with the life of the person remembered such as the badge of the Royal Engineers or the Royal Air Force.

This church contains bits and pieces of almost all of our different building styles. The Saxon period is said to be represented by the re-use of some of the earliest materials in the tower and some would have it that the arcade to the chancel is a typical Saxon feature, although this, of course, could be a later reproduction. There is Norman work in the Ham stone of the nave along with one of the nave windows which is in the Early English style. Much of the inside has been rebuilt including the chancel walls. In the wall to the right of the north door are two tomb recesses, the one nearest the door, dating from around 1300, is the effigy of a lady wearing a wimple lying beneath a trefoiled gable arch with two smaller attendants by her head. The smaller recess has an effigy of a knight and dates from the late fourteenth century.

The five bells in the tower were increased to six in 1992 when a treble weighing $5\frac{1}{4}$cwt was added. The number one bell is inscribed 'First I call to wake you all,' three and five bear the inscription 'Health and delight good ringing yields.' The belfry tower screen is dedicated to Dorothy Ellen Fletcher who died in office in 1972 having been headmistress of the village school just outside the church gates for fourteen years.

Every village should have a ghost story and Ashill is no exception, in fact it has six. Seven if you count the corpse inside the coffin which six phantom bearers carry through Nunnery Wood towards St Mary's. They have been seen, whether after those who have seen them have just left the Ashill Inn is not on record.

Further north of Ashill, and also bypassed by the A358 there is little to attract one at Hatch Beauchamp except Hatch Court and the grave of Colonel Chard the VC hero of Rorke's Drift in the Zulu War.

The manor of Hache at the time of Domesday, and like so much of this part of Somerset, was owned by Robert, Count of Mortain who leased it to Robert Fitz Ivo (the Constable). When the lands of the Count of Mortain were forfeited to the crown in 1092 Hatch passed to Robert Beauchamp and it stayed in the family's hands until 1361 when John Beauchamp died without issue and Hatch passed through marriage

Somerset County Council workmen tarring a road in south-west Somerset during the 1920s.

to the Seymour family. The Seymours, an important family in medieval England, became even more important when Jane Seymour became the third wife of Henry VIII and Edward Seymour, who was created Duke of Somerset, virtually ruled the country as Lord Protector during the minority of Edward VI (1547-53) until his execution in 1552. But Hatch stayed in the hands of the Seymour family until 1676 when, again through marriage, it passed to the Bruce family. It went through several hands after that, including those of John Collins who had Hatch Court built in 1755.

In the churchyard of St John the Baptist's church, which stands behind Hatch Court, the marble tomb of Colonel John Rouse Merriot Chard looks just as new a century or more later as when it was first placed there It can be found by the south door below the Chard window. Lieutenant Chard became a national hero in 1879 when he was in command of a body of eight officers and 131 soldiers, 35 of them in sick quarters, who were building a bridge beside the mission house at Rorke's Drift when they came under attack by over 3,000 Zulus. The enemy, fresh from their overwhelming victory at Isandhlwana where a force of 800 British soldiers had been slaughtered were eventually driven off and a large scale invasion of Natal prevented. Chard saw further service in Singapore and Cyprus before retiring, as a Colonel, to Hatch Beauchamp where his brother, Revd Edward Chard, was the rector. He died unmarried in 1897 at the age of fifty and, such was his standing in England at a time when good, old-fashioned jingoism was at its best, that Queen Victoria sent a wreath as 'a mark of admiration and regard for a brave soldier from his Sovereign.' Today, of course that part of the Zulu War is best remembered because of the film *Zulu* which ends with a recitation of the eleven VCs awarded afterwards. One to Lieutenant Chard, seven of the others to members of the 2nd Battalion, 24th (Warwickshire) Regiment of Foot.

St John's church is late medieval and, mostly built of blue lias, stands on the site of an earlier building of which record remains. The oldest part of the church is the much altered chancel, the nave, the tower and the north aisle being from around 1500.

It always well worth reading a visitors book in any church, but especially so at St John's were many of the visitors turn out to be either former members of the Royal Engineers or from South Africa including, on occasion, some from Rorke's Drift.

The RAF's wartime station at Merrifield is near Ilton, two miles east of Ashill on the other side of the usually crowded A358. It was from there, barely minutes into Tuesday, 6 June 1944, almost 100 fully laden C47 transport planes (the Douglas Dakota, the workhorse of the Second World War) took off and, still gaining height, woke most of the residents of Ilminster as they headed south towards the English Channel and beyond.

They were the first of two assault waves heading for Normandy (operation Albany) where their human cargo would drop on and around the tiny French village of St Mère Église to secure the area for the glider-born troops that would follow. Today the main N13 road bypasses St Mère Église as it heads towards Bayeaux and Caen. But it is still worth the small detour to visit the village and see the uniformed mannequin permanently entangled on the church roof as John Steele was in real life on that June morning all those years ago. Now dead, he made the occasional return to his one moment of fame which was so vividly portrayed in the film *The Longest Day*. Merrifield was originally built as a bomber station and was used until1960 when it was sold off. In 1972 it re-opened as HMS *Heron* and is now used for helicopter pilot training for the aicrews at the nearby RNAS at Yeovilton.

John George Hayman, the first of the five generations of a baking family that has supplied much of the area around Ilminster with its daily bread, actually began his life as a baker while serving as such in the Royal

Known as the 'Hedgehog', this unusual contraption was used to pick up apples from the floors of apple orchards in south-west Somerset after they had either dropped or been shaken from the trees.

The post office, Silver Street, Barrington, in the 1930s.

Navy in the later years of the nineteenth century. He came to settle in Wheelwright House, Ilton, in 1891 and set up in business at nearby Bullens Farm where a bakery was already in existence. When he died in 1919 his son Frederick sold his own bakery in West Street and moved to Ilton to carry on the family business at Bullens Farm In the 1930s the third generation of the family, Frederick's sons Leslie and Norman began baking and did so until 1965 when Leslie's son Tim and his wife Jenny, became the fourth generation Ilton's baking family. For a spell they opened a baker's shop in Chard and it was there that one could see many of the cakes decorated to a very high standard by their daughter Claire, the fifth generation of the family. Those who have had the pleasure of sampling Hayman's bread will learn with regret that bread in no longer made in Ilton and that the old bakery no longer exists. It was completely demolished at the turn of the century and replaced by a thatched bungalow constructed of imitation Ham stone.

This imitation stone does weather in time but, during its early years, it does tend to depress one. But there is a lot of the real thing at Ilton, especially around St Peter's parish church and the village green. Well worth a visit are Merrifield House and Ilton Court which stand hard by. Not to be missed are the Wadham almshouses near the church and the

Barrington Club Day, c. 1900.

Whetstone's almshouses on the road to Stocklinch that were founded in 1642 and have attractive, three-light mullion windows.

Barrington, its name stems from its being 'the settlement of Barra's people, is a gem. It has that almost but not quite untidy look that one comes to expect from a working village, especially in Somerset. Thatch and gabled Ham stone abounds in all directions and, of course, Elizabethan Barrington House, now the property of the National Trust. Although not particularly tall the central tower at the church of St Mary the Virgin soon catches the eye because of its crenellations and its unusual octagonal shape, one of only twelve such towers in Somerset. There is a peal of six bells, the sixth, dated 1894 bearing the name of Taylor, a Loughborough bell founder, is inscribed 'Let them be numbered with the Saints' and was tolled when a parishioner died. The oldest is the fifth bell which is dated 1743 but bears no inscription. Also worth noting is the stoup for holy water to the right of the fifteenth-century porch.

There would have been a Saxon church on its site and, in time a chapel of ease to the Mother Church at South Petherton, Barrington not being mentioned in Domesday (1086) when it was possibly part of the manor of its bigger neighbour. Inside St Mary the Virgin both the north and south transepts retain their squints which allowed the worshippers in them to see the altar, the south squint being much larger than its northern neighbour and there is a piscina in the south dating back to 1300. Even older is the tracery of the window there. Often, some might say almost always, the hands of the Victorian restorers ruined much of the splendours that were the English village churches. Not at St Mary the Virgin, however, where the restoration of 1859-61 did nothing but good. The south aisle, part of the restoration, became known as the 'women's aisle' because husbands and wives separated after entering the church.

There is a brass plate to the memory of Edith Bond who died in 1939 after sixty-two years as organist there.

Just outside the church, Pound Cottage - its name tells us what it once was - is an attractive mixture of Ham stone, white colour wash and thatch and the usual pleasures of a lunch time half are made all the more enjoyable because of the lovely surroundings of the Royal Oak inn which has been there since at least the eighteenth century but the name might well come down to us from an earlier time. The many Royal Oaks dotted around the countryside are said to taken their name (after the Restoration in 1660) from the fact that Charles II hid in an oak tree to escape his pursuers after the Battle of Worcester (1651). But, if he hid in all the oak trees he is said to have done, it is a wonder he ever reached the coast at Charmouth, let alone found time to hire a boat for France.

Barrington Court lies just outside the village if you leave by Water Lane which has more than its fair share of the village's better houses. Built on the site of an earlier building, it was inherited in 1514 by Henry Daubneney who was created Earl of Bridgwater in 1538. He began the present building, but due to his extravagance and his subsequent disgrace following the trial and death of Catherine Howard in 1542, which led to his bankruptcy, it was only after 1552, when the estate was bought by William Clifton, a London merchant, that the house was completed. In 1605 Sir Thomas Phelips bought the house but sold it in 1625 to William Strode, a Shepton Mallett clothier. It was his son, another William, that built the enormous, brick stable block next to the main house which is now known as Strode House.

The Duke of Monmouth is never far away in this part of Somerset, it was only seven miles to the north that his rag-tag-and-bob-tail army met its end at Sedgemoor 1685. A few days before the battle the Duke was entertained at Barrington by William Strode, junior, but the house

115

Barrington, c. 1907. Looking eastward towards the Royal Oak from the small green in front of the pound and the parish church.

stayed in the Strode family until 1745. A coincidence considering that was the year that James II's grandson, Bonnie Prince Charlie, raised the flag of rebellion on the shores of Loch Shiel.

Passing through many subsequent hands, it became National Trust property at a cost of £11,500. In 1920, the sugar magnate Col. Arthur Lyle took a ninety-nine-year lease on the property. The National Trust had found the initial cost of maintaining the property too high, in 1991 Andrew Lyle, Col. Lyle's grandson, had the same problem and he relinquished the lease to the National Trust. It is well worth the entrance fee if only to admire the lovely gardens in spring and summertime.

Ruskway Lane, which connected Barrington with the Westport Canal, along with the village's main street, became a turnpike in 1823 when it was taken over by the Ilminster Trust and a toll house built at the junction of the two roads. The Westport Canal was, a two-mile branch of the canal system around Taunton, the Parrett and the River Isle. Westport was a purpose-built community but the canal lasted only thirty-five years before closing in 1875. Much of the warehousing remains today.

Barely a mile as the crow flies, probably two along the narrow, steep-banked lanes, Shepton Beauchamp takes the first part of name from sheep farm (there is a Sheep Lane there), the Beauchamp came later when the family of that name arrived in the middle of the twelfth century. Later the male line of the Beauchamp's ran out and the estate

Watergore, the tiny hamlet on the line of the old A303, just over a mile from South Petherton and Shepton Beauchamp, c. 1910.

passed through marriage to the Seymours who built a manor house (since demolished) on the way towards Barrington. It is possible that Sir John Seymour, one-time Sheriff of Somerset, lived there in the middle of the sixteenth century. If so it is possible that his young daughter Jane also spent some time in Shepton Beauchamp, later, of course, she became the third wife of Henry VIII and the mother of Edward VI, Henry's only legitimate son.

Egg Shackling may never become an Olympic sport, but it is big stuff in Shepton Beauchamp on Shrove Tuesday when each child brings an egg which is put in a sieve and shaken, the winner is the egg that is remains unbroken at the end.

The village was granted a market by Henry III in 1260 and, despite no market being held there since around the nineteenth century, the name Shambles is retained to this day in Shepton Beauchamp. Pictures as recent as 1910 show that a man was employed to sweep a crossing there and, like much of the village, the Shambles has one to 2ft-high pavements in case of flooding.

Said to be thirteenth century, St Michael's parish church stands in the centre of the village. Built mostly of lias and Ham stone and very attractive despite the Victorian rebuilding of the south aisle which, like its northern neighbour, dated from the fourteenth century around the same time as the chancel. The roof was more or less replaced in 1952 due to the damage caused by the death watch beetle. There are eight bells in the 70-ft tower, the oldest dated 1738. One of the bells bears the inscription, 'Hang me right and ring me well, they'll hear my sound on Hamdon Hill.'

A few yards from St Michael's the popular Duke of York public house takes it name from James II (1685-88) when he was Duke of York. It was originally based in another house close by but later moved into its present home. Shepton Beauchamp's other pub, the New Inn at the corner of Church Street and Buttle Lane, closed around the 1960s. Its old Fives court is still there.

The Seavingtons, St Mary's and St Michael's, lie to the east of Ilminster on the gentle slope that rises from the Lopen brook to the A303 trunk road which now bypasses both of the tiny villages. So tiny in fact that it was felt that there was not enough 'support' for two churches and, after local opinion had been sounded, the church at Seavington St Mary, St Mary's church of course, was closed in 1983. A wise choice no doubt, St Michael's is easily the largest of the two places, but a pity in so much that St Mary's is by far the better of the two buildings. St Mary's was taken under the wing of the Churches Conservation Trust in 1984 and is still visitable although you have to walk two hundred yards to get the key. It is well worth the walk.

The Duke of York, Shepton Beauchamp, c. 1902. Today the handsome sign and the gas light are no longer there, while the cottages opposite have been almost rebuilt in Ham with tiles.

Although much of the interior has been removed the shell of the church and its wagon roof retains its beauty. Among the things that are still there is a font which suggests that there was already a church here during the Norman period. The present building, however, dates from the thirteenth century, the west tower and porch following around 1500. There were originally three bells dated 1621, the work of George Purdue of Taunton. One of the three was recast at the beginning of the twentieth century when three new bells were added.

Unusually so, the floor of the pews are lined with red bricks. Some of the tiles on the roof are of Ham stone.

Not only is the church at Seavington St Mary the better of the two, at the risk of starting an internecine war it must be added that the village is also the prettier. One of the best houses being thatched Littlefield which, at first blush, appears to have been built from Ham stone rubble but, in fact, come from a similar local stone The southern end of the building was once a medieval open hall. Opposite, Littlefield Barn was once part of the same farming complex. A few yards away the solid, Georgian Manor Farm is also well worth a second look.

Seavington St Michael's church stands away from the village towards the Lopen Brook which loops to the south of the village where it crosses the Fosse Way which runs between the two villages and Lopen. The

Shepton Beauchamp, c. 1905, looking from Middle Street into Church Street.

The old Forge, Shepton Beauchamp, c. 1900. The space on the left was the site of the village pound.

oldest part of St Michael's is the twelfth-century nave, the chancel being added in the thirteenth.

A yew tree in the churchyard has a girth of around ten or eleven feet which, because yew (*texus baccata*) is said to grow around a foot in diameter every century, suggests that it might be the oldest part of the church.

Whether Swan Thatch, a late seventeenth-century building in the middle of the village, takes it name from the two thatched swans on the ridge of the thatched roof or, those swans were placed there because of the name, is open to question. What is certain is that is was once a bakehouse but became the village post office.

Donyatt is not spoilt by the fact that the A358, and the heavy traffic heading towards Chard, East Devon and West Somerset from the M5, pass right through the middle of the village. It has too attractive a 'city centre' for that, although regulars at the George looking out at those heavy vehicles might sometimes wonder if they will safely negotiate the dog-leg bend outside or finish up in the bar. A public house has stood on this site for over 200 years but, in the 1930s and after a disastrous fire, the building was moved about twelve-fifteen feet back from the road.

The fifteenth-century St Mary's parish church is behind the George and well worth a visit, if only to admire the remarkable cheerful air that the clerestory and the mostly clear glass windows lends to its interior. On one of the window ledges is the stone head of a lady wearing a wimple, a type of head dress that dates from the twelfth century so, presumably, it came from an earlier building

On the tower that peeps up over the surrounding buildings, the clock face was reguilded in 1959, much of the cost being met by donations from lorry drivers who relied on the clock, which can be seen from a considerable distance, for the correct time.

There is stoup outside the now closed west door which, in pre-Reformation days, contained the Holy Water with which worshippers blessed themselves before entering the church. Entry is now by the south door, both doors still having their original locks and keys. The alabaster reredos is in front of a colourful east window, the oak pulpit, on a stone pedestal, is Jacobean, but the pews are Tudor with the bench ends from an even earlier period, the Tudor connection stemming from the visits of Henry VIII (1509-47) to hunt at nearby Park on occasion.

Blocking the front view of the church from passers-by in Church Lane, the superb Dunster almshouses date from 1624, a gift of Lord Dunster for 'three old ladies and three old gentlemen'. At the end, and roughly opposite the old school, is the master's house. Opposite the almshouses another very attractive row of buildings were originally four farm labourers cottages but have been converted into two.

If Swift was to rewrite his *Gulliver's Travels* and site Lilliput in England, he could easily change the Lilliputian war which saw the Bigendians insist everyone should break their eggs at the large end into one between Somerset and Devon. Then the bone of contention would be which county made the best cider. Neither, or rather both, would win. Sadly less and less of the real stuff is made today, more and more orchards being grubbed out as manufacturers change over to cheaper imported apples although a few farmers make 'scrumpy' for their own consumption. It is not uncommon to see the odd rat's head or tail seen sticking out of the cheese on floors in barns that would never pass the brassy eye of the EU gauleiters in search of things to ban. But, as any back-door cider maker will tell you, the odd rat or mouse in the cheese is what gives the cider 'it's bite.'

It is produced commercially through Somerset, and where better than at Dowlish Wake where the Perry Cider Mills still use the old traditional local apples, including such favourites as Yarlington Mill, Dabinetts, Somerset Red Streak, Tremletts Bitter, and Kingston Black.

The New Inn, Dowlish Wake, a building thought to date from 1760. The pub was originally called the Three Horseshoes but, with conscious humour we hope, it was renamed the New Inn.

They mostly come from Perry's own eleven-acre orchard or from local farmers. Sadly the 'king' of cider apples, the great Tom Putt. is seldom available these days.

More than one Tom Putt became rector of Gittisham near Honiton in Devon, and one of them is credited with the introduction of the apple that bears his name. Probably it was the Thomas who was born in 1757 and has his claim supported in a stained window at Farway church, a few miles from Gittisham, where he was the vicar for a spell. The grubbing out of the orchards when cider manufacturers, unwisely, changed to foreign imports, turned Tom Putt into an endangered species almost overnight. Happily a Gittisham man, Nelson Owen, laid down some fresh trees and the famous apple is making a slow recovery.

At Perry Mills there is an interesting museum containing artefacts of both farming equipment and barrels and other cider memorabilia. Of course there is cider on sale. It is good as well – and who better to recommend it than Winston Spencer Churchill, one time MP and Prime Minister, who, in 1945, wrote to William Churchill, uncle of the present owners of the cider mills but no relation to the great wartime premier, thanking him for the gift of excellent cider received via Lord Beaverbrook, who owned the nearby Cricket Malherbie estates, and commenting on its excellence.

The cider industry runs along an age-old calendar that is as unchanging as the seasons themselves. The year starts on 6 January, the traditional date for Wassailing which is still celebrated in many parts of Somerset. The tradition comes down to us from our ancestors who were seeking for fertility in their orchards and prosperity from its produce. Shot guns are fired into the air, trees are beaten with branches to awaken the spirits who been slumbering since the previous harvest and the cider from the harvest tested for the first time. Traditional songs, handed down from generation to generation are sung as the wassailers dance around the trees. In other words an excuse, if one was ever needed, for a good old-fashion knees-up and a sampling of what is left from last year's brew.

General maintenance begins as Spring approaches, trees are pruned and tidied up in readiness for the next crop and, sadly more often today with so many of our old orchard grubbed out in the name of progress, replanting is necessary as well.

Like all types of farming, the cider industry is at the mercy of the weather, especially in May when severe frosts could decimate the blossom and endanger that Autumn's harvest. Traditionally the three nights around the 21 May are known as Frankan nights when the blossom is said to at its most vulnerable. To assist in pollination many cider makers put bee hives in their orchards. Looking for fallen apples in long grass could be a problem. The answer is to mow the grass regularly during the summer, either mechanically or with sheep.

A Hutchings and Cornelius coach standing outside the church at Barrington, where the Cornelius half of the company started out in the coaching business around 1946. The firm later moved to South Petherton.

In late summer the first apples are ready. These are generally the eaters with Beauty of Bath among the earliest – and the best. The cider apples are ready by October, the time when the industry is at its busiest, although 'tree-shaking' has been largely replaced by hand-pickers or by mechanical means. The first cider, which is ready by Christmas, is that made from Morgan Sweet apples. Which is the best cider? The one that you like the best of course.

Dowlish is a lovely village, lots of cheerful Ham stone and thatch and delightful buildings, none more so than the Dower House which looks at the old pack horse bridge and the ford beside which is now piped under the road but there is a channel there to carry the overflow in rainy weather. Beside the bridge, Bridge Cottage is well worth a second look, and so, a few yards away, is Manor Cottage. Just above the parish church, Mount Cottage, is handsome Ham stone on three sides, but the front is plastered and colour washed.

St Andrew's, the third church on this site, stands on a small mound looking down on its charges and out across the valley towards the distant heights of Windwhistle. Outside, the well weathered and rugged Ham stone walls and tower blend well with the surrounding trees. Happily the tower escaped the restoration of 1861-62, when the original stone was mostly re-used. Otherwise the nave and aisle inside were not greatly

South Petherton Hospital, c. 1950.

improved. The most interesting monument inside is probably that of Isabel Wake who died in 1359. She lies low down, with a pet dog at her feet, beside the steps to the Speke chapel. She brought the manor of Dowlish with her on her marriage to John de Keyne; and it was their daughter Joan, who took the manor on to the Speke family when she married John Speke. Effigies of John, in armour, and Joan lie side by side on a table tomb in the Speke chapel where memorials to many other members of the family adorn the walls. Perhaps the most interesting one, certainly to recent generations of visitors, is the monument to John Hanning Speke, the man who discovered the source of the Nile.

Elsewhere in St Andrew's there is a well worn Norman font, much stained glass, much of it as memorials to members of the Speke family, and an attractive, if new, wagon roof ceiling. The earliest known rector is Adam de Sanford (1316).

John Hanning Speke was born near Bideford in North Devon, on 4 May 1827, and went to Barnstaple grammar school. His father, William Speke, who regularly turned down requests from William Pitt, the Prime Minister, to seek election as an MP, married Georgina Hanning, a member of a wealthy merchants' family from Dillington, to the east of Dowlish Wake and towards Dinnington. In time William Speke inherited the family seat at Jordans just outside Ilminster, and it was from there in 1844 that the seventeen-year-old John entered service with the East India Company, being recommended by no less a person that the ageing Duke of Wellington.

Eventually the thrill of India palled for him and he headed back to home in Somerset. The journey took him a year, the wanderlust that he had developed taking him, via Aden, to explore Central Africa with Sir Richard Burton. In Somalialand he was captured by natives, staked hand and foot on the ground and stabbed several times with spears, two of the wounds coming when spears were thrust through both his thighs. He recovered and was soon back in the bosom of his family but, bitten again by the wander bug, he went off to the Crimean War and then back to Central Africa, again with Burton, with whom he eventually fell out when he suspected that the latter was trying to claim the credit for discovering the source of the Nile. Their appetites had been whetted by rumours of a huge lake. Leaving from Zanzibar, it took them fifteen months to reach Lake Tanganyika where Speke parted from Burton and went on alone in search of the mysterious lake. On 9 June 1858, he

125

Yeabridge, South Petherton, c. 1912.

stood looking down at Lake Ukerewe (renamed Lake Victoria by Speke in honour of the great Queen). It was huge as well and, at over 26,000 square miles, is the second largest fresh water lake in the world.

He returned to England but, at the request of the Royal Geographical Society, went back to Victoria Nyanza to make certain it was indeed the source of the Nile. He did so but there was considerable argument, particularly from Burton, that he wrong and it was not until 1871, seven years after Speke's death, that Henry Stanley, of 'Dr Livingstone I presume' fame, was able to confirm the source of the 4,160-mile-long river was Lake Victoria or, to be more exact, its head stream, the Kagera.

Tragically Speke was accidentally shot, on 15 September 1864, at a partridge shoot near Corsham in Wiltshire, and died almost instantly aged only thirty-seven years. He was brought back to Dowlish Wake and buried in the recently rebuilt St Andrew's. Among the mourners was Dr David Livingstone.

The area to the east and north of Lake Victoria became a British protectorate (a euphemism for possession) in 1894 and was given its independence in 1962. After the last Union Flag to fly on the shores of Lake Victoria was lowered it was brought back to England and laid up near Speke's tomb in St Andrew's parish church in the presence of the Ugandan High Commissioner Mr T.B. Bazarrabusa and the Information Attaché Mr L.Okot.

Acknowledgements

We are greatly indebted to Vic Matravers for so generously allowing us to use many of his fine collection of Somerset postcards and pictures from which most of those in this book came from. Thanks are due also to the *Chard & Ilminster News*, which has faithfully recorded Chard's history since 1874, especially the staff who are even more charming, helpful and courteous than duty demands, and to Philip Evans, the editor of *Pulman's Weekly News*. Both papers have readily made their files available to us. Also the staff at Tempus Publishing, especially Matilda Pearce, who has been a tower of strength.

Others to have helped us or made available some of the pictures in this book are Frank Huddy, who also wrote the excellent introduction, Jack Helliar, Roy Poole, of Numatic International, Edna Gillard, Doug Tucker, Gerald Thompson, fortunate enough to live in the Dunster almshouses at Donyatt and who took the time and trouble to tell us a bit about the village, Ann Saville for her memories of Crewkerne, Gerry Smith and John Martin.

Rob Stacey of Chaffcombe took the time to tell us about the history of that village, and followed us three miles to Cricket Malerbie because, when we returned the keys of the church to him, we absent-mindedly gave him a set of our car keys instead of those of the church. To be fair to us, Rob just as absent-mindedly took them.

Bibliography

Foot, David, *Sunshine, Sixes and Cider, The History of Somerset Cricket*, David & Charles, Newton Abbot, 1986.

Chard History Group, *John Stringfellow 1799-1883*, Jay Print & Design, Chard, 1999.

Clancy, Kevin, *A History of Chard Cricket Club 1841-1991*, LGC Chard, 1991.

Hadfield, Charles, *The Canals of South West England*, David & Charles, Newton Abbot, 1957.

Guy, John, *Mr Bird and his Infirmary Crewkerne Hospital, 1866-1904*, privately published, 1984.

Hawkins, Mac, *Somerset At War*, The Dovecote Press, Wimborne, 1988.

Pearce, Patricia, *Seventeen Cum Sunday, Barrington's Story*, Axminster Printing Works, Axminster, 1993.

Pevsner, Niklaus, *The Buildings of England* (South and West Somerset), Penguin Books, Hamondsworth, 1958.

Phillips, Melanie, *The Divided House*, Sidgwick and Jackson Limited, London, 1980.

Warren Derrick, *Dening of Chard*, The Somerset Industrial Archaeological Society, Taunton, 1989.